COOKING WITH CURTIS

easy, everyday and adventurous recipes for the home cook

curtis stone

photography by Craig Kinder

PAVILION

CONTENTS

INTRODUCTION

I have written this book to try and pass on a little bit of knowledge about ingredients that I feel typify what each season has to offer. It's so important to eat food that's as locally grown as possible and in season. Do you remember when your mother used to say "strawberries don't taste like they used to". It comes as no surprise that the strawberries she missed were locally grown, in season and ripe. However, these days it's hard to keep track of what's in season and what's not. I think this is particularly so when you live in a big city and are dependant on supermarkets who for some reason think that it's necessary to stock every type of fruit and veg all year round. This means that we have to transport food long distances, in some cases around the world, which in turn results in over-priced produce that is not as fresh as it should be.

So in this book are 24 of my favourite ingredients split into their seasons, with 3 recipes for each ingredient. And because I completely understand that people are sometimes pushed for time I have split the recipes up into 3 categories to make it easier. The colour key shown below appears at the top of each recipe and will tell you whether it is "easy", "everyday" or "adventurous".

For some reason, nowadays we are not listening to our instincts and I have no idea why. I think that Mother Nature did a pretty good job when she worked out which ingredients belong to which seasons and I'm hoping that by the time you get to the end of this book, you'll agree!

Ever since I was young I have always been fascinated with food. Whether it was making marmalade with my Nan and Granddad or fudge with my Granny, I look back now and think it was a little odd for a 5-year-old to be so obsessed with food. That obsession continued throughout my teenage years until I began to cook as an apprentice chef at the Savoy hotel in Melbourne. During my time there I was lucky enough to work with a few European and British chefs who pointed out that you were no-one in the cooking world until you had made your way in Europe. So, as someone who loves a challenge, I packed my bags. After seeing a little of what Italy, France and Spain had to offer I arrived in London. When I first arrived I needed money pretty quickly as I had overspent on my travels, so day one in London was spent job hunting.

The first cookbook that I was ever given was called *White Heat*, written by Marco Pierre White, the infamous chef who was the youngest man in the world to be awarded 3 Michelin

● ○ ○ **EASY** represents recipes with only 5–6 ingredients and should take no more than 20 minutes to prepare and cook.

● ● ○ **EVERYDAY** these recipes should be achievable on an everyday basis, include about 6–8 ingredients and take less than 1 hour.

stars. His restaurant was the first door I knocked on that day and to my disbelief I began working that afternoon at his restaurant, The Grill Room, Café Royal. The first few months were trying to say the least. We worked from 9am until midnight, with the occasional break in the afternoon, from Monday to Friday. On Saturdays I worked midday to midnight which meant I only had Sunday off. To top it off I didn't get paid for over a month and as a result had to sneak on the tube to get to work while sleeping on the floor of a mate's pub. This went on for around 9 months until Marco opened a new restaurant called the Mirabelle. I was sent there and after a couple of months we were awarded a Michelin star and I was made Sous Chef. I stayed at the Mirabelle for a further year before Marco decided to move me to Quo Vadis, one of his flagships in Soho, London. It was here that I was made Head Chef for the first time. In only a few years my life had kind of flashed past my eyes.

It was while I was at Quo Vadis that I was first approached by a publisher who phoned to say they were publishing a book about London's finest chefs. To my amazement they wanted to include me in it. I nearly fell over because to be included in the company of people I had always admired was not only a little surreal, but also incredibly humbling. When the book was published I had been at Quo Vadis for around 4 years. After the release of the book came a number of opportunities within the media. To me it was quite funny being asked to appear on television, but then it's like anything – the more you do the more comfortable you feel. I was then lucky enough to be asked to co-host a show called "Surfing The Menu" with my mate, Ben O'Donohue. In the show we got the opportunity to travel around Australia and meet loads of passionate food producers and cook with their produce. This was the first time in my adult life that I was not attached to a restaurant and cooking everyday for paying customers. It was a dream come true, being paid to travel and cook my way around a country that I love.

While this is a lot of fun, it has also enabled me to get back in touch with the product at its rawest form. To me the most important thing about cooking is not years of skill or practice, but understanding what you are cooking. I think you only need a little bit of knowledge about an ingredient and then you will understand how to handle it. I also firmly believe that if you use the right ingredient at the right time of year it's hard to go wrong. So get stuck in and get cooking!

● ● ● ADVENTUROUS

the type of recipe that you cook to impress someone. It may take an hour or more and even call for some exotic ingredients.

SPRING

To me, spring is one of the most exciting changes of season. We are coming out of the colder weather and everybody starts to get out and about again. It feels natural that in spring our diets become a little lighter.

One of the first signs of spring is the asparagus that suddenly floods our markets. When this happens I go absolutely mad for it, as I do for spring lamb which is younger and leaner than that available later in the year. I also like to

eat a lot more fish in general, but especially prawns and tuna. Early spring peas fresh from a local grower seem to taste far sweeter than any available later in the year. Wild garlic leaves become available and I put them into everything from light salads to mashed potato.

I grew up in Melbourne, Australia, which in spring hosts the Melbourne Cup, a horse race that is part of the Spring Racing Carnival. This carnival lasts for around a week and involves a lot of champagne and a lot of social light eating, not to mention the lovely weather. To me this is what spring should be – a celebration of early sunshine and what that brings to our tables … light, flavour-filled food.

One thing I love about living in London is the amazing parks and gardens that everybody can enjoy. When the daffodils and tulips blossom there is no better place to head with a picnic basket full of spring's offerings.

ASPARAGUS

The asparagus season only lasts for around three months. English asparagus is slightly smaller than that grown in mainland Europe, although I believe the English variety has the best flavour.

Asparagus grows white beneath the ground. Once the shoots grow through the earth, the plant begins to produce chlorophyll, which turns it green. If any difference in taste exists, white asparagus is more intense in flavour.

When selecting spears, the tips and buds should be tightly closed. It is somewhat heat sensitive so once picked it needs to be chilled immediately. If not, the tips and buds will begin to open and the natural sugars start to decrease. It will also cause the spears to become tough and stringy.

When preparing asparagus it is best to trim the woody portion of the stem. If it is large and the skin tough you may have to peel the stem from about half way down.

High in vitamin A, C and E, it is rich in soluble fibre, potassium and iron and low in sodium and fat.

● ○ ○　WHITE ASPARAGUS SAUTÉED IN BROWN BUTTER WITH A FRIED EGG

36 white asparagus spears, peeled
salt
3 tbsp butter
4 hen's eggs
5 tbsp tarragon vinegar

serves 4 as a starter

I love the flavour of white asparagus, and when combined with the nutty flavour of burnt butter it's a marriage made in heaven. This dish is so easy to make as the egg yolk also acts as a sauce. It's great for brunch or as a starter at dinner.

Poach the asparagus in a saucepan of boiling salted water for 2–3 minutes until just cooked.

Heat a large frying pan. Add 2 tbsp butter and allow to turn a light brown colour. Add the asparagus and leave to caramelize for about 2–3 minutes. Remove the asparagus from the pan once it is a deep golden brown colour and place 9 spears on each serving plate.

Add 1 tbsp butter to the same pan, and fry the eggs to your liking. Place on top of the asparagus spears.

Deglaze the pan with the vinegar, then spoon around the plates and serve.

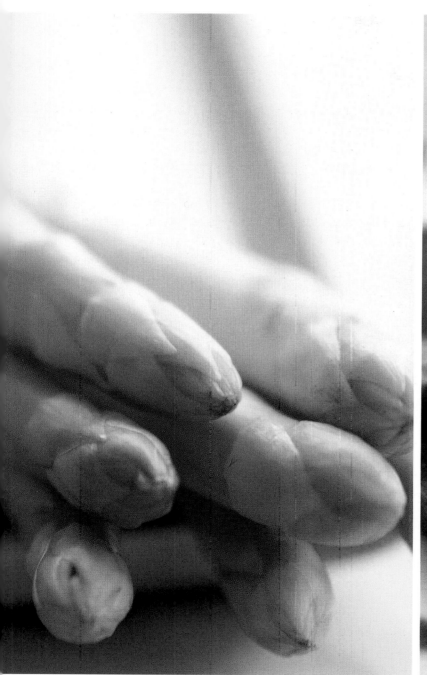

SALAD OF ASPARAGUS AND MARINATED ARTICHOKE WITH FRESH GOAT'S CHEESE

These marinated artichokes are available at all good delis and even some supermarkets, which make them the essential option when time is an issue. Their distinctive flavour stands up to the strong taste of the goat's cheese and is a lovely balance with the asparagus.

To make the dressing, place the vinegar in a large bowl then while constantly whisking slowly add the olive and sunflower oils until combined. Add half the chives and mix well.

Blanch the green asparagus in a saucepan of fast-boiling salted water for 2–3 minutes then refresh immediately in ice cold water.

Place the asparagus, artichokes, salad leaves and chervil in a large bowl and mix together.

Drizzle the dressing over the salad, and toss until combined. Distribute the salad evenly between 4 serving plates.

Shape the goat's cheese into 4 quenelles using 2 spoons dipped in warm water and place on top of the salad. Alternatively, simply slice the goat's cheese. Drizzle any remaining dressing around the outside of the plates, garnish with the remaining chives and serve.

For the dressing

4 tbsp white wine vinegar
4 tbsp extra virgin olive oil
4 tbsp sunflower oil
2 tsp fresh chives, finely chopped

For the salad

20 green asparagus spears, cut
  6 cm/2½ inches from tip
salt
6 marinated artichokes, cut into
  8 pieces
100 g/3½ oz mixed salad leaves
8 fresh chervil sprigs
160 g/5½ oz soft goat's cheese
  (any type without rind will
  be suitable)

serves 4 as a starter

● ● ●

STEAMED JOHN DORY
WITH A GREEN ASPARAGUS SAUCE

The reason that this recipe has made its way into the adventurous category is simply because the sauce will take a while to complete, however, it can be made in advance or even the day before. The rest of the dish is really simple and let's face it, with the combination of asparagus, morels and steamed John Dory...it's worth it!

For the sauce
butter
1 shallot, sliced
3 button mushrooms, sliced
1 fresh thyme sprig
1 bay leaf
375 ml/13 fl oz white wine
375 ml/13 fl oz double cream
28 green asparagus spears,
   peeled and trimmed
¼ bunch of fresh flat-leaf parsley

100 ml/3½ fl oz water
100 g/3½ oz butter
200 g/7 oz fresh tagliatelle
salt and freshly ground
   black pepper
20 small morels
4 x 180 g/6½ oz John Dory fillets

serves 4 as a main course

To make the sauce:

Melt a little butter in a medium saucepan. Add the shallot, mushrooms, thyme and bay leaf and sweat gently without colouring. Pour the wine into the pan and stir to deglaze, then reduce the liquor by half. Add the cream and bring to a near simmer then strain, pour back into the pan and return to the heat.

Add the asparagus trimmings and parsley leaves to the sauce and cook for 3–5 minutes. Meanwhile, place a bowl in the freezer until it is cold. As soon as the sauce is cooked, pour it into the cold bowl and chill immediately. If the sauce is not cooled straightaway, the end result will be a dull green-brown colour. Once the sauce is cool, transfer to a blender and process for 2 minutes, then strain, pour into a small saucepan and slowly warm.

Bring the water to the boil in a medium saucepan. Place the butter in a pan and gradually whisk in 4 tbsp of the boiling water to form an emulsion. Split into 2 pans (½ in each), set aside, but keep warm.

Cook the tagliatelle until *al dente* (tender but still firm to the bite) then drain, add to one of the pans of emulsion, season with salt and pepper and keep warm until ready to serve.

In the other pan of emulsion, cook the morels for 2 minutes and keep warm until required.

Season the fish with salt and pepper then place in a bamboo steamer with the asparagus spears and steam for 5 minutes.

When ready to serve, coat the tagliatelle with some of the reserved emulsion then arrange in the middle of 4 plates. Lay the steamed fish over the top of the pasta and garnish with the asparagus spears and the reserved morels.

Foam the sauce with an aerolatte or hand-held blender and spoon onto the plates. Garnish with parsley sprigs and serve.

TUNA

Despite the fact that tuna is a fish that is not seasonal, I have included it as a spring ingredient because it's light flesh is great to eat in warmer weather.

Tuna lives in warm waters all over the world and is enjoyed in nearly every type of cuisine. It is a large fast-moving fish that when caught can weigh in at anywhere from 10–700 kilograms. Its flesh has high blood-content levels which not only give it its rich red appearance but also enables the fish to swim at speed.

There are five varieties of tuna, the three most commonly available are yellow fin, albacore and blue fin. However, blue fin tuna is now an endangered species and so should be avoided at all costs.

Tuna cuts come from the loin or the belly (also known as torro). The loin, which is much darker in colour and makes up a much larger percentage of the fish's flesh, is more commonly available than the belly. The belly has a larger fat content (although it is comparitively still lean) making this cut very popular in Asian markets where it is most often eaten raw.

When purchasing tuna it is important to look for a deep red colour with a clean bright sheen. The tuna should be firm to touch and should have quite a neutral smell. It cannot be eaten too fresh.

Tuna should never be over-cooked – medium rare is best – as its low fat content can cause it to become dry.

High in protein, vitamin A and D and omega-3 fatty acids.

SASHIMI OF MACKEREL AND TUNA
WITH A PONZU DIPPING SAUCE

While Asian food isn't usually my bag, this dish is so easy that someone with no experience can get it right. All you need to do is make sure you purchase the very best tuna and mackerel and the job is done for you!

For the mackerel:

Sprinkle half the table salt on a baking tray. Place the mackerel on top and sprinkle the remaining salt on top of the mackerel, to cover. Cover with cling film and place in the refrigerator for 2 hours.

Rinse the mackerel under cold running water to wash off the salt and place in a shallow dish. Pour the vinegar over and leave to marinate for 4 hours.

Remove the mackerel from the vinegar and pat dry on kitchen paper. Gently remove the skin from the mackerel and slice the flesh thinly.

Slice the tuna thinly.

For the dipping sauce:

Combine the soy sauce, yozu sauce and sesame oil in a small bowl and mix together thoroughly.

Serve the sashimi of mackerel and tuna on a platter with raw vegetables, such as carrot and mooli julienne, the dipping sauce and wasabi, if you like. Garnish with some fresh coriander leaves.

75 g/3 oz table salt
2 x 80 g/3¼ oz mackerel fillets
175 ml/6 fl oz rice wine vinegar
250 g/9 oz fillet sushi-grade tuna

For the dipping sauce
50 ml/2 fl oz Japanese soy sauce
2 tbsp yozu sauce
5 drops sesame oil

To serve
2 carrots, julienne
10-cm/4-inch piece mooli,
  julienne
wasabi (optional)
fresh coriander leaves

serves 4 as a starter

● ● ○

HERB-CRUSTED TUNA CARPACCIO WITH AVOCADO AND BABY HERBS

600 g/1¼ lb sushi-grade tuna
2 tbsp extra virgin olive oil
30 g/1 oz fresh herbs (chives,
   dill, chervil and tarragon),
   coarsely chopped
2 ripe avocados, diced
juice of 1 lemon
2 tbsp fresh chives, chopped
½ fresh red chilli,
   de-seeded and finely chopped
salt and freshly ground
   black pepper
30 g/1 oz fresh baby herbs
juice of 1 lemon
50 ml/2 fl oz olive oil

serves 4 as a starter

Whenever you get the chance to buy lovely fresh tuna, there is nothing better than eating it raw. The combination of ripe avocado, lemon juice and fresh tuna is an old one but it is still extremely hard to beat.

Using a sharp knife, trim the tuna into a round shape discarding the sinewy flat side of the tuna loin.

Heat a non-stick frying pan. Add 2 tbsp olive oil and sear the sides of the tuna evenly while making sure not to sear the ends. Remove the tuna from the heat and leave to cool.

Spread the chopped fresh herbs out on a plate. Roll the seared sides of the tuna loin in the herbs and wrap firmly in a few layers of clingfilm. Leave to rest in the refrigerator for at least 1 hour.

Meanwhile, combine the avocado, lemon juice, chives and chilli (chili) in a medium-sized bowl and season with salt and pepper.

In a bowl, dress the baby herbs with lemon juice and olive oil, reserving a little of the oil for drizzling.

Thinly slice the tuna and season lightly with salt. Layer the slices on each serving plate with the avocado and baby herbs. Drizzle a little oil on the side of each plate and serve.

ESCALOPE OF TUNA WITH AUBERGINE PURÉE AND CITRUS DRESSING

● ● ●

Even though this recipe is classified as adventurous, it can be very quick and easy if you make the aubergine purée well in advance. It will keep in the refrigerator overnight and can be easily reheated in a small saucepan before serving.

To make the aubergine purée:

Preheat oven to 140°C/275°F/Gas Mark 1. Slice the aubergines in half, cut 3 slits each way into the aubergine without piercing the skin and place on a baking tray. Sprinkle the salt over the aubergines and leave for 20 minutes to extract the bitter juices, then rinse quickly under cold running water. Pat dry, sprinkle the aubergines with half of the lemon juice, all the garlic, olive oil and thyme then wrap individually in foil and place in the oven for 1 hour.

When the aubergines are ready remove from the oven and scrape out the flesh, discarding the seeds. Chop the flesh into small pieces, place in a bowl and mix with the remaining lemon juice and the basil.

For the citrus dressing:

Combine the lemon juice and coriander seeds in a bowl, then, while whisking constantly, slowly add the olive oil. Pour the dressing into a small saucepan, add the tomato and caperberries and warm gently.

Blanch the baby fennel in a pan of boiling salted water for 2–3 minutes, drain and add to tomato and caperberries. Keep warm.

To cook the tuna:

Preheat a griddle pan or light a barbecue. Season the tuna with salt and pepper and rub all over with a little olive oil then cook in the pan or on the barbecue for 60 seconds on each side.

Place the aubergine caviar in a small saucepan and warm over a low heat. Add the basil and coriander to the remaining dressing and stir well.

Arrange a pile of tomatoes, caperberries and fennel on 4 serving plates. Place the tuna on the tomato mixture and drizzle the dressing around the plate. Using 2 spoons dipped in water, place a quenelle of aubergine purée on top of the tuna and serve.

For the aubergine purée

2 aubergines

20 g/¾ oz salt

juice of 2 lemons

2 garlic cloves, peeled and thinly sliced

125 ml/4 fl oz olive oil

4 fresh thyme sprigs

1 tbsp fresh basil, finely sliced

For the citrus dressing

50 ml/2 fl oz lemon juice

10 coriander seeds, toasted and crushed

150 ml/5 fl oz olive oil

6 tomatoes, blanched, peeled, de-seeded and cut into strips

20 caperberries

8 baby fennel bulbs, trimmed

4 x 160 g/5½ oz tuna escalopes

salt and ground black pepper

50 ml/2 fl oz extra virgin olive oil

½ cup fresh basil leaves

30 fresh coriander leaves

serves 4 as a main course

PRAWNS

Prawns are fished all year round and work very well with other light spring ingredients. While there are numerous species of prawn of fresh and salt water variety, the prawns that I have used in the following recipes are 'king' (or 'tiger') simply because they are the most easy to find.

Prawns are filter feeders so should be sourced from clean unpolluted waters. They inhabit the warm waters of the Indo-Pacific region and have long been considered a delicacy.

When choosing prawns look for bright shells and firm tails. They should smell of the ocean and, if raw, should be dark green in colour. Avoid prawns with darkness around the head as this can indicate that it has aged. Prawns should be cooked as fresh as possible (thus many prawn trawlers nowadays either cook them out at sea or freeze them immediately after being caught). It is also important to not overcook prawns as the tails will become tough.

Prawns are high in iron, zinc and Vitamin E, protein and calcium, low in saturated fat and have good levels of omega-3 fatty acids.

● ○ ○ ## BBQ KING PRAWNS WITH OLIVE OIL, LEMON JUICE AND FRESH PARSLEY

20 king prawns, cut in half
lengthways with shell on
4 tbsp extra virgin olive oil
2 small fresh chillies, finely
chopped
zest and juice of 3 lemons
2 tbsp fresh flat-leaf parsley,
coarsely chopped

serves 4 as a starter

No matter where Aussies go in the world, they get teased with "throw another prawn on the barbie". Here I'm doing just that and I can tell you it's nothing to be ashamed of. In fact, it shows how something so simple can taste so good.

Preheat a barbecue or griddle pan to a high heat.

Drizzle the prawns with a little olive oil and place them, flesh-side down, on the barbecue or into the pan and cook for 30–60 seconds. Turn the prawns over, add the chilli, lemon zest and parsley, and squeeze over the lemon juice.

As soon as the prawns are cooked to a solid, white colour (about another 30–60 seconds), remove from the heat, drizzle a little extra olive oil over them and serve immediately.

PLATTER OF FRUIT DI MARE
WITH RASPBERRY VINAIGRETTE

It must be because I'm an Aussie but I just get so excited about eating good seafood in this way. It doesn't really matter what type of seafood you cook, as long as it's fresh and there's some cold champagne nearby; it will always be a winner.

To make the raspberry vinaigrette:

Place the vinegar and chopped dill in a bowl and while whisking constantly slowly add the grapeseed and olive oils until blended. Season with salt and pepper and leave the dressing to chill in the refrigerator until required.

For the platter:

Place the carrot, celery and onion in a large saucepan of water and bring to the boil.

Add the prawns to the pan, cover and cook for about 3 minutes until firm and red in colour. Remove from the pan and chill in the refrigerator.

Wash the clams and mussels under running water until no sand or weed remains.

Heat a large saucepan and add olive oil. Add the shallot and garlic and sweat briefly, about 1–2 minutes. Add the clams, mussels, parsley and white wine to the pan, cover and cook until the mussels and clams open. Remove from the pan and place on a flat tray to cool down. Discard any that remain closed. Once the mussels and clams are cool, place in the refrigerator until ready to assemble the platter.

Fill a large deep-sided platter or ice bucket with crushed ice. Arrange the seafood on top, including the freshly shucked oysters. Serve with the dressing on the side, the lemon to squeeze over and some fresh crusty bread, if you like.

50 ml/2 fl oz raspberry vinegar
¼ bunch of fresh dill, finely chopped
50 ml/2 fl oz each of extra virgin
  olive oil and grapeseed oil
salt and freshly ground black
  pepper
1 carrot, peeled and chopped
1 celery stick, chopped
1 onion, peeled and chopped
12 prawns
2 tbsp olive oil
1 shallot, finely diced
1 garlic clove, peeled and crushed
400 g/14 oz fresh clams
400 g/14 oz fresh mussels,
  beards removed
¼ bunch of fresh parsley stalks
1 tbsp fresh flat-leaf parsley,
  finely chopped
50 ml/2 fl oz white wine
plenty of crushed ice
12 oysters
1 lemon, cut in half
crusty bread, to serve (optional)

serves 4–6 as a starter or main
  course

● ● ● # KING PRAWNS WITH CARAMELIZED ENDIVES AND ENDIVE FOAM

2 endives

For the endive foam

55 g/2¼ oz butter

250 g/9 oz endive trimmings

2 tsp sugar

4 tsp honey

500 ml/16 fl oz vegetable or fish
   stock

250 ml/8 fl oz double cream

24 king prawns, peeled and
   de-veined

sea salt and freshly ground black
   pepper

juice of ½ lemon

serves 4 as a starter

Endives are a European vegetable that if not treated carefully can be quite bitter. Try this recipe and see just how good endives can taste if slowly cooked and matched with a beautiful ingredient like king prawns.

To cook the endives:

Tie the endives together with string and cook in a large pan of water for 2 hours at 60°C/140°F to eliminate any bitterness from the endives. If you don't have a thermometer, the water should be just below a simmer.

To make the endive foam:

Melt 20 g/¾ oz of the butter in a large heavy-based saucepan. Add the endive trimmings, sugar and 2 tsp honey and allow to caramelize until soft and golden brown. Add the stock and leave to simmer for 10 minutes. Add the cream and bring to a near simmer then remove the pan from heat and leave to cool. Transfer the sauce to a blender and process briefly, then pass through a fine sieve and return to a clean saucepan to reheat while you prepare the rest of the dish.

Once the endives are cooked through, remove from the pan and leave to cool.

Cut each endive in half lengthways and drizzle each half with the remaining honey.

Heat a large saucepan and melt another 20 g/¾ oz of butter. Add the endives and leave to caramelize. As soon as they are golden brown, about 5 minutes, turn them over and cook for a further 1 minute.

Melt the remaining butter in a separate non-stick frying pan. Add the prawns and sauté for about 2 minutes. Season with sea salt and black pepper and add the lemon juice. Remove from heat and divide between 4 serving plates with the endive halfs.

Briefly whiz the endive sauce to a foam with a hand-held blender and drizzle over the plates to serve.

LAMB

Lamb is eaten by most cultures and religions around the world causing it to be one of the most heavily farmed animals. For a sheep to be considered lamb it must be less than 12 months old while spring lamb should be between 4 and 10 months.

After slaughter it is important that lamb is hung and aged. It is hung as full carcasses to improve both flavour and texture.

When purchasing lamb look for meat that is light pink and fat that is pearl-like white. It is essential that you choose the cut of lamb to suit the dish. Tougher cuts, like the shoulder, are more suited to stews and braises whilst more tender cuts of the meat, like loins and rumps, are better suited to roasting and grilling. Unless being used in a stew, lamb should be cooked to a pink colour.

Lamb is high in zinc, iron and protein and is rich in vitamin B.

● ○ ○

ROAST RACK OF LAMB WITH A HONEY AND ROSEMARY CRUST

6 slices bread, stale or dry
½ bunch of fresh rosemary, leaves
  only, chopped
salt and freshly ground
  black pepper
30 g/1 oz melted butter
2 x racks of lamb with 6 cutlets,
  boned
1 tbsp runny honey
1 tbsp Dijon mustard

serves 4 as a main course

Roasting meat on the bone brings a great element of flavour to a dish. Because racks of lamb are so lean, I think if you make a crust the meat is protected from the heat and stays much juicier. What better combination than lamb, honey and rosemary.

Preheat oven to 190ºC/375°F/Gas Mark 5. Place the dry bread in a food processor and pulse until breadcrumbs form. Add the chopped rosemary and season well with salt and pepper. Add the melted butter, mix together, then transfer this crust mixture to a shallow dish.

Heat a large frying pan and seal the lamb on all sides then remove. Mix the honey and mustard together in a small mixing bowl and spread over the lamb. Dip the glazed lamb into the crust mixture until completely covered and cook in the hot oven for 12–15 minutes, depending on the size of the lamb.

Leave the lamb to rest for 4–5 minutes, then carve and serve.

ROAST RUMP OF LAMB WITH BRAISED SPRING PEAS AND MORELS

● ● ○

This is a real celebration of spring flavours. Peas, morels and lamb are all perfect in spring and when you eat the three together the marriage of flavours is too good to be true. I use a rump of lamb because it has a great balance of fat and flavour.

To make lamb sauce:

Heat a large heavy-based pan and add olive oil. Add the lamb trimmings and sauté for 5–10 minutes until golden brown. Remove the lamb trimmings from the pan and pour off the excess fat. Return the trimmings to the pan with the shallot and herbs and sauté for 1 minute. Add the red wine to the pan and stir to deglaze, then reduce the liquor to a glaze. Add the stock and reduce the sauce by half.

Strain the sauce through a sieve into a small saucepan and while whisking constantly slowly add the extra virgin olive oil.

For the lamb:

Preheat oven to 190°C/375°F/Gas Mark 5. Heat a non-stick frying pan, add oil and seal the lamb rumps on all sides. Transfer to a roasting dish and cook in the hot oven for 12–15 minutes.

Meanwhile, place the balsamic vinegar in a small pan and reduce to a glaze.

Remove the lamb rumps from the oven and leave to rest for 4 minutes. Place the chopped herbs in a shallow dish. Brush the top of the lamb with the balsamic glaze and press the glazed surface into the dish of chopped herbs.

Heat a small saucepan and add oil. Fry the crushed garlic briefly without colouring. Add the morels and fry for 60 seconds, then add the peas, a ladle of the lamb sauce and a ladle of water and stir. Add the knob of butter, stir to combine and cook for 2–3 minutes.

Slice the lamb into 3 pieces, drizzle with the sauce, season with salt and pepper and serve with the peas and morels.

For the sauce

60 ml/2 fl oz olive oil
300 g/11 oz lamb trimmings
1 shallot, finely sliced
1 fresh thyme sprig
1 bay leaf
150 ml/5 fl oz red wine
800 ml/1¼ pints lamb stock or
    water
1 tbsp extra virgin olive oil

4 x 220 g/7½ oz lamb rumps
2 tbsp olive oil
200 ml/7 fl oz balsamic vinegar
2 tbsp fresh mint, finely chopped
2 tbsp fresh flat-leaf parsley,
    finely chopped
1 tbsp olive oil
2 garlic cloves, crushed
100 g/3½ oz morels, cut in half
250 g/8 oz fresh peas
a knob of butter
salt and freshly ground
    black pepper

serves 4 as a main course

● ● ● **WARM SALAD OF SMOKED LAMB, WITH A CABERNET SAUVIGNON VINAIGRETTE**

2 tsp Maldon sea salt

2 tsp paprika

½ tsp crushed black pepper

2 x 250 g/8 oz loins of lamb

For the vinaigrette

75 ml/2½ fl oz Cabernet
   Sauvignon vinegar

1 tbsp fresh chives,
   finely chopped

50 ml/2 fl oz grapeseed oil

50 ml/2 fl oz extra virgin olive oil

20 g/¾ oz tea leaves

20 cherry tomatoes

80 g/3¼ oz mustard cress

80 g/3¼ oz wild rocket

40 g/1½ oz mixed salad leaves

serves 4 as a starter

Smoking incorporates flavour in a way that is quite unusual. It can be as strong or as mild as you like. In this particular recipe the smoke flavour is very mild as I don't want it to overpower the delicate lamb flavour.

To cure the lamb:

Rub the salt, paprika and crushed black pepper over the lamb loins and leave in the refrigerator for 2 hours.

To make the vinaigrette:

Place the vinegar and chives in a mixing bowl and while whisking constantly slowly add the grapeseed and extra virgin olive oils. Set aside.

Preheat oven to 200°C/400°F/Gas Mark 6. Line the base of a double saucepan with foil and place over a high heat. As soon as the foil is very hot add the tea leaves. Once the tea leaves start smoking, place the lamb loins in the top of the double saucepan, replace lid and leave for 45 seconds. Remove the saucepan from heat and allow the smoke to infuse the lamb for a further 5 minutes.

Meanwhile heat a frying pan. Remove the lamb from the top of the saucepan and seal the lamb on all sides in the hot pan.

Place the cherry tomatoes on a baking tray and place in the hot oven for 5 minutes. Remove and leave to cool.

Thinly slice the smoked lamb. Toss lamb together with the tomatoes, cress, rocket and salad leaves. Divide between 4 serving plates and pour vinaigrette over. Serve immediately.

CHAMPAGNE

I will never forget the first time I tasted champagne and felt those gorgeous tiny bubbles on my tongue. It was quite a sweet champagne and I was very young. I know most kids hate the taste of any alcohol but I was hooked.

I am happy to say that I am still obsessed. I also love this small region of northern France and worship the 17th-century Monk, Dom Pérignon, who first mastered the process of capturing the sparkle in the bottle. It is a highly skilled art. The bubbles are kept in the wine through a secondary fermentation. A little yeast and sugar are added to the wine before sealing the bottle and this yeast settlement is removed after 2 or 3 months and the bottle is re-corked.

I have always hated the term cooking wine. Please don't use cheap and nasty tasting wine in your food, as the dish will only taste as good as the ingredients you put into it.

If you are making a desert you are best to use a slightly sweeter champagne which is indicated by "sec" or even "demi sec". "Brut" will indicate a dry style of champagne suitable for savoury dishes.

ALPHONSO MANGO BELLINI

4 ripe Alphonso mangoes, peeled
with flesh trimmed from stone
1 bottle champagne

Serves 4–6 as an apéritif

My best mate Chris Sheldon runs a bar in Soho, London called Zebrano. It was here that I was introduced to the legendary bellini made with white peach purée and Prosecco. Here I have modified a mango purée and I hope you enjoy the results.

Place 4 champagne glasses in the freezer to chill. Place the mango flesh in a blender and purée until smooth. Push the purée through a fine sieve into a bowl and place in the freezer or over ice to chill.

Remove purée from the freezer when ice cold. Stir gently while slowly adding the champagne until incorporated.

Pour into the chilled champagne glasses and serve immediately.

OYSTERS WITH CHAMPAGNE
AND CAVIAR

Well what can I say? These three ingredients speak for themselves. Any one of them on their own is amazing but all of them together is totally orgasmic!

Melt a little butter in a medium saucepan, add the shallot and sweat until soft. Add the champagne and reduce by two thirds. Add the cream and bring to a near simmer then add any juice from the oysters.

Strain the sauce through a sieve into a saucepan and return to the heat for 30 seconds. Do not allow the sauce to boil.

Add the oysters to the sauce and leave to poach for 20 seconds then remove the pan from the heat leaving the oysters in the sauce for a further 30 seconds. Remove the oysters from sauce and place back in their shells. Arrange on serving plates. Use a hand-held blender to foam the sauce. Add the caviar to the sauce, spoon over the oysters and serve.

1 shallot, peeled and sliced
10 g/¼ oz butter
250 ml/8 fl oz champagne
100 ml/3½ fl oz double cream
1 tbsp oyster juice (if any from the oysters)
24 oysters, shucked, shells reserved
30 g/1 oz oscietre caviar

serves 4 as a starter

● ● ●   # STRAWBERRY AND CHAMPAGNE JELLY

For the strawberry jelly
3 leaves gelatine
250 g/9 oz strawberries
25 g/1 oz caster sugar
50 ml/2 fl oz champagne
For the champagne jelly
8 leaves gelatine
750 ml/1¼ pints champagne
50 g/2 oz caster sugar
4–6 strawberries, hulled

cocktail sticks

serves 4–6

If you intend to impress your guests with a presentation like this, be prepared to spend a couple of fiddly hours in the kitchen. If, however, you're pushed for time, you can simply chop the strawberry and set it in the champagne jelly for a more rustic look.

To make strawberry jelly:

Soften the gelatine in a small bowl of cold water (about 250 ml/8 fl oz). Place the strawberries and sugar in a blender and process until a purée forms. Push the purée through a fine sieve into a small saucepan, discarding the seeds and gently warm over a low heat until it is slightly warmer than room temperature.

Place the 50 ml/2 fl oz of champagne in a separate small saucepan and gently warm over a low heat. Add the gelatine and allow to dissolve. Slowly pour the warm champagne into the warm strawberry mixture, stirring to combine. Set aside until required.

To make champagne jelly:

Soften the gelatine in a little cold water (as above). Place the champagne in a medium saucepan and slowly bring to a gentle simmer over a low heat for 1–2 minutes. Add the sugar and gradually add the softened gelatine, stirring constantly to ensure that there are no lumps. Remove the saucepan from the heat and leave to cool until the mixture is about room temperature.

To assemble the jelly:

Pour a small amount of the strawberry liquid into each glass and leave to set in the refrigerator (about 2 hours, or until jelly is firm).

Place a cocktail stick horizontally into each of the 4 hulled strawberries and rest on the rim of each glass.

Half-fill the glass with the champagne liquid and return to the refrigerator.

Once the champagne jelly has set (about 1 hour), remove the glass from the refrigerator and gently and carefully remove the cocktail sticks. Fill the glass with the rest of the champagne liquid until the strawberry is just covered and return to the refrigerator for a further hour.

Once the jelly is set, spoon 4–5 tbsp of the strawberry jelly over the champagne jelly and leave to set again (about 2 hours).

The jelly may be served in the glass or the glass can be dipped into hot water and the jelly turned out of the glass onto a serving plate.

RHUBARB

Rhubarb is another ingredient that is particularly seasonal, available from late April to late June. Historically, the rhubarb plant was more commonly used as an ornamental plant, but we can thank the Brits for bringing it in to the kitchen. Although it is used as a fruit and made into sweet pies, puddings and crumbles it is actually a vegetable and can also be used as a savoury item.

It is quite an easy vegetable to grow and if you know someone that grows it in their veggie patch I always think its nice to trade a bunch of rhubarb in return for a pot of jam. If, like me, you live in a big city like London and the closest veggie patch is 50 miles away, try to buy rhubarb that still has firm, crisp stems and does not look too wilted.

When you prepare it, cut off and discard the leaves (which are poisonous due to a high level of oxalic acid). The stems will take up to half an hour to cook and can be prepared by baking, stewing and poaching to mention but a few methods. It is naturally quite acidic so you will need to cook with quite a bit of sugar.

High in fibre, calcium, potassium and sodium and vitamin C and very low in fat.

● ○ ○ RHUBARB AND STRAWBERRY JAM

6 large sticks rhubarb, coarsely chopped
4 punnets strawberries, hulled juice of 1 lemon
1 vanilla pod, split lengthways
150 g/5 oz/3/4 cup caster sugar
buttered, crusty bread, to serve

Makes 2 x 300 ml/½ pint jars

My mum still grows rhubarb in her vegetable garden as she did when I was younger. While I was writing this book, I had to phone dear "Lozza" and ask her for a good recipe as she is the guru when it comes to jams. I hope you agree.

Place the rhubarb, strawberries, lemon juice, vanilla pod and caster sugar in a large, heavy-based saucepan and cook over a medium–high heat for 90 minutes, or until the fruit begins to thicken or set.

Test that the jam is ready by placing a small amount on a saucer and leaving in the refrigerator for 5 minutes to set. Meanwhile, sterilize the jam jars with boiling water.

Once jam is ready, transfer to the sterilized jars and leave to cool before covering with a lid or serving.

Serve with buttered crusty bread.

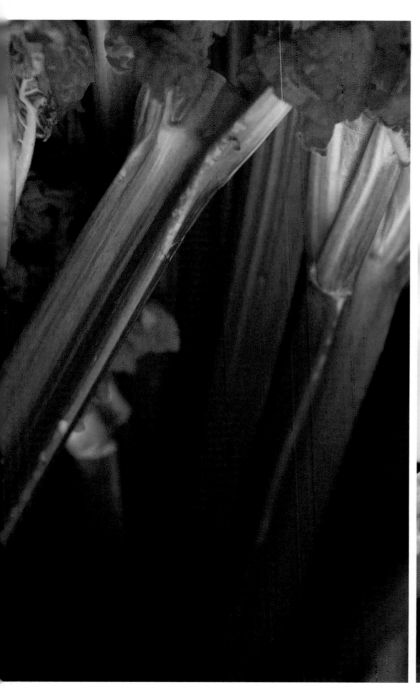

BAKED RHUBARB
WITH A COINTREAU GRATIN

The Cointreau gratin is simply a sabayon (emulsion) made from egg yolks, some sugar and liquor, in this case cointreau. This recipe is quite adaptable and will work with almost any alcohol even white wine, so why not try it with your favourite.

Preheat oven to 180°C/350°F/Gas Mark 4. Place the rhubarb in a small roasting tin and lay the vanilla pod on top. Sprinkle the butter over the rhubarb and cover the tin with foil. Cook in the hot oven for 10 minutes.

Remove the tray from the oven and rub the vanilla pod between your fingers to massage some of the vanilla seeds from the pod onto the rhubarb. Replace the vanilla pod on top of the rhubarb, re-cover with foil and return to the oven for a further 15–20 minutes (cooking time may vary depending on ripeness and woodiness of the rhubarb).

Place the egg yolks, sugar, water and Cointreau in a large, heatproof bowl and start to whisk together. Place the bowl over a small saucepan of boiling water and continue whisking until the mixture resembles a sabayon. This will take about 4–7 minutes and should resemble a lighter and fluffier version of whipped cream.

Place the rhubarb on individual serving plates and spoon over the sabayon. Using a culinary blowtorch, quickly brown the sabayon for 30 seconds. If you don't have a blowtorch, place under a preheated hot grill for about 1–2 minutes until light golden brown. Serve immediately.

4 rhubarb sticks, cut into
  6 cm/2½ inch lengths and
  halved lengthways
1 vanilla pod, split lengthways
20 g/¾ oz butter, finely diced
3 egg yolks
75 g/3 oz caster sugar
50 ml/2 fl oz water
75 ml/2½ fl oz Cointreau

serves 4–6

ROAST DUCK WITH RÖSTI POTATOES AND RHUBARB AND RED PORT SAUCE

For the sauce

25 g/1 oz caster sugar (quantity may vary depending on sharpness of the rhubarb)

3 rhubarb sticks, coarsely diced

60 ml/2 fl oz red port

150 ml/5 fl oz chicken stock

For the rösti potatoes

4 large baking potatoes, peeled

salt

leaves of 2 fresh thyme sprigs

1 tbsp olive oil per rösti

2 x 360 g/12½ oz large duck breasts

200 g/7 oz baby spinach, stems removed and washed

20 g/¾ oz butter

serves 4 as a main course

Duck is one of my favourite meats. It's very rich and needs something with a little sharpness to cut through the strong flavour. Duck with orange has always been a popular dish and in the same way the acidity of the orange works with the duck, so does rhubarb.

To make the sauce:

Place the sugar and rhubarb in a medium pan and cook over a slow–medium heat for 5 minutes. Add the port and bring to the boil for 2 minutes. Add the chicken stock and cook, stirring frequently, until rhubarb resembles a sauce, about 10–15 minutes.

To make the rösti potatoes:

Preheat oven to 180°C/350°F/Gas Mark 4. Using a Japanese mandolin, finely grate the potato then sprinkle it with salt and place in a large dish towel or cloth. Squeeze all the moisture out from the potatoes through the cloth then transfer the potatoes to a bowl. Mix in the thyme leaves then place in a small bellini pan, about 2-3 cm/¾–1¼ inch in depth (alternatively you can use a frying pan and a mousse ring or round pastry cutter, placing the potatoes inside the ring).

Using 1 tbsp olive oil each, cook the rösti potatoes in batches over a medium heat until golden brown on one side. While the rösti is cooking, constantly push the potato down with a fork. Turn over and continue to cook until it is golden on both sides. The rösti potatoes can be made in advance and reheated to serve.

Place the duck breasts skin-side down in a frying pan over a medium–high heat and cook until skin is light golden brown, about 1½–2½ minutes. Place in the hot oven for 8–12 minutes. Make sure that the skin does not become too dark.

Remove the duck from the oven and leave to rest for 4–5 minutes.

Meanwhile, sauté the spinach in a little butter in a separate saucepan until soft. Using the back of a slotted spoon, squeeze out the excess moisture from the spinach and keep warm until required.

When ready to serve, place the spinach and rösti potatoes on 4 serving plates, slice the duck and fan around the spinach and potato. Drizzle the sauce around the plate and serve.

SUMMER

When summer finally arrives everybody seems to have a smile on their face. For some it's the thought of holidays and for others, taking the convertible out for a drive. It's the perfect time of the year to get *al fresco* dining into full swing.

To me summery food should be clean and simple – nice crisp tastes which suit the sunshine. The barbecue is the perfect vehicle to cook on as it lets you be outside with your friends and family rather than shut up in the kitchen. As

the day lasts so much longer than in colder months it is important to make the most of it.

This is the time when broad beans are at their best and there are so many things you can do with them – little salads, soups or veggie dishes. Peppers are also in season and are very adaptable. If you have never tried it before, make this summer the first time you make a cold soup. Summer fruits and vegetables are fantastically refreshing, so lovely ripe tomatoes, summer berries, fennel and watercress should all make an appearance.

This is when I think the heavier meats should come off the menu – it should be all about seafood, poultry and fish. Sauces are much lighter and dressings and vinegars can be used in their place. Summer is also a time to share food – large platters of antipasti and pre-prepared nibbles are great to share with friends.

MOZZARELLA

It was not until I moved to the UK and tasted mozzarella brought directly from Italy that I realized how amazing it can be. As a youngster growing up in Australia I always thought of mozzarella as a rubbery tasteless cheese. I now understand that was because there is a serious art to making it. Mozzarella should be made from the milk of buffalos and when you speak to a buffalo farmer he or she will speak at length about how their particular regime of exercise and feed results in premium quality milk. I have even had one old Italian farmer tell me that he sings to his animals.

Making the cheese involves separating the curds and the whey and pouring water (around 60°C/140°F) over the cheese and moulding the balls by hand. This may sound easy enough but believe me it is not. The cheese then needs to be stored in the whey, or some salted water, to keep its softness.

The general rule of thumb when buying fresh mozzarella is the softer the better. You should also eat the cheese very fresh, if it's been in the fridge for more than 4–5 days then use this for cooking and buy some more to eat fresh.

High in saturated fat, low in sugar and a good source of protein, calcium and phosphorus.

● ○ ○ SALAD OF TOMATO AND MOZZARELLA

4 ripe plum tomatoes
12 ripe cherry tomatoes
2 tbsp white balsamic vinegar
2 tbsp extra virgin olive oil
2 tbsp fresh basil leaves, ripped
4 balls buffalo mozzarella,
    drained
16 leaves rocket
salt and freshly ground
    black pepper

Serves 4 as a starter

In order for this dish to be great the tomatoes have to be perfectly ripe and the mozzarella fresh and soft. I was once told by an Italian buffalo mozzarella producer that the mozzarella should not come into contact with metal as it would compromise the taste. I'm not sure if this is true, but when you tear a mozzarella ball using your hands, the texture is just beautiful.

Coarsely chop the plum and cherry tomatoes and mix together with the vinegar in a large bowl. Add the olive oil and mix again with three-quarters of the ripped basil.

Place the tomatoes in the centre of each serving plate.

Tear the mozzarella into small chunks and arrange over the tomatoes. Drizzle with extra virgin olive oil, garnish each with a basil sprig and a few rocket leaves, season with salt and plenty of black pepper and serve.

DEEP-FRIED AUBERGINE AND MOZZARELLA WITH BASIL

This is a great snack or can be served as a canapé with this fabulously spicy tomato sauce. It's important to salt the aubergine as this draws out the natural bitterness but it is also equally important to wash off the salt.

For the tomato sauce:

Sweat the shallots in a little olive oil until soft.

Add the garlic and chilli and leave to sweat for a further 1 minute. Add the tomatoes and cook for 15–20 minutes.

For the aubergine:

Slice the aubergine thinly into 16 rounds and lay on a baking tray. Sprinkle the salt over the aubergines and leave to stand for 10 minutes to extract the bitter juices then rinse under cold running water and pat dry with kitchen paper.

Slice the mozzarella into 8 pieces then make a sandwich with the aubergine, mozzarella and basil leaves.

Dip the aubergine sandwich into the flour and shake off any excess. Then dip into the beaten eggs and then into the breadcrumbs to coat. Repeat the process to give the sandwich a double coating of the breadcrumbs.

Heat the oil in a deep saucepan to 160°C/325°F (or until a cube of bread browns in 30 seconds). Carefully lower the sandwich into the hot oil and deep-fry until golden brown, about 2–3 minutes. Drain on kitchen paper and cut the sandwich into 4 portions. Serve with a warm tomato sauce.

For the tomato sauce

2 shallots, peeled and diced

2 tbsp olive oil

2 garlic cloves, peeled and crushed

1 fresh chilli, chopped

10 ripe plum tomatoes, skin removed, finely diced

1 aubergine

2 tbsp salt

1 ball buffalo mozzarella, drained

8 fresh basil leaves

100 g/3½ oz plain flour

2 eggs, lightly beaten

150 g/5 oz fresh breadcrumbs

1 litre/1¾ pints vegetable oil, for deep-frying

warm tomato sauce, to serve

serves 4–6 as a canapé

● ● ●

HOMEMADE PIZZA WITH MOZZARELLA, CHERRY TOMATOES AND COPPA

For the pizza base

500 ml/16 fl oz water,
  at room temperature
20 g/¾ oz easy-blend dried yeast
100 ml/3 fl oz extra virgin olive oil
1.1 kg/2½ lb Italian "OO" flour,
  plus extra for dusting
75 ml/2½ fl oz milk
25 g/1 oz salt

20 cherry tomatoes
sea salt and cracked black pepper
4 tbsp olive oil
2 tsp fresh oregano, chopped
2 white onions, peeled and sliced
2 x 250 g/8 oz cans plum tomatoes
salt
sugar, to taste
100 g/3½ oz Italian cured meat,
  such as *coppa*
1 ball buffalo mozzarella
wild rocket leaves

serves 4–6 as a main course

It might seem strange that a pizza has found its way into my adventurous category. It seems so simple and if you buy a pizza base, it is. But when making one from scratch some people may find the base requires patience and practice. Good luck!

For the pizza base:

Pour the water into a large bowl and add the yeast, olive oil and half of the flour and mix well. Add the milk, salt and the rest of the flour and mix to form a soft dough. Knead the dough until smooth and elastic, about 10–15 minutes. Place in a large oiled bowl, cover and leave to stand in a warm place until doubled in size.

Break off about 175 g/6 oz (size of small apple) of the dough and roll out on a work surface to the desired size. Alternatively, the dough can be rolled out into any shape or size as long as it remains thin.

To semi-dry the cherry tomatoes:

Preheat oven to 110°C/230°F/Gas Mark ¼. Cut the cherry tomatoes in half, season with salt and pepper and drizzle with 2 tbsp of the olive oil. Sprinkle the oregano over then arrange on a baking tray and place in the oven for 1½ hours.

To prepare the coppa:

Place the *coppa* on a baking tray and cook in the preheated oven for 5–7 minutes, or until crispy. Cool, then break into small pieces.

For the tomato sauce:

Heat a large saucepan, and add 2 tbsp olive oil. Add onions and sweat until soft. Add the canned tomatoes and simmer gently for 20–30 minutes. Season with salt and sugar to taste.

To assemble the pizza:

Increase the oven temperature to 220°C/425°F/Gas Mark 7. Place the rolled dough on a large flat baking tray and cover the base lightly with the tomato sauce. Sprinkle the base with all the toppings and place in the hot oven for 10–12 minutes. When the pizza is ready to serve, garnish with wild rocket leaves and serve.

GARLIC

Garlic bulbs are in season in late spring and summer. In spring you can buy wild garlic leaves for salads and stir-fries. It's my belief that garlic should be used subtly, so not to overpower other flavours (done in Italy by sautéing it in olive oil and then discarding it so as only to flavour the oil). Or slowly cook whole cloves as I do in the pork belly recipe. You will be amazed at how delicate garlic can be.

Regular consumption lowers blood pressure and reduces the risk of heart attack or stroke. It also has anti-bacterial effects. Good source of manganese, selenium, B6 and vitamin C.

● ○ ○ LINGUINI WITH GARLIC, ANCHOVIES, WHITE WINE AND PARSLEY

250 g/9 oz dried linguine

50 ml/2 fl oz olive oil

1 shallot, peeled and finely diced

2 garlic cloves, crushed

20 anchovy fillets, finely chopped

20 extra fine capers

10 stoned green olives, coarsely chopped

250 ml/8 fl oz white wine

100 ml/3½ fl oz extra virgin olive oil

2 tbsp fresh flat-leaf parsley, coarsely chopped

salt and black pepper

20 anchovy fillets

flat-leaf parsley sprigs

serves 4–6 as a starter or main course

When choosing anchovies try not to buy the salted ones, as they may be good in sauces but if you use them in a dish like this, they will overpower the other ingredients. The ones you want are lightly marinated in olive oil.

Cook the linguine in a large saucepan of salted boiling water for 10–12 minutes, or until *al dente* (tender but firm to the bite).

Heat the olive oil in a large frying pan. Add the shallot and sweat until soft but not coloured. Add the garlic and cook for a further 30 seconds then add the chopped anchovies and cook for 1 minute.

Add the capers and olives then pour the white wine into the pan and stir to deglaze. Add the olive oil.

Drain the cooked linguine and add it to the frying pan with the sauce. Toss in the chopped parsley and season with salt and pepper.

Place in a large serving bowl, garnish with anchovies and parsley sprigs and serve.

PAN-FRIED SALMON WITH GARLIC, BROAD BEANS AND BEURRE BLANC

I find salmon has a richness that most fish don't have, which means it can easily stand up to the strong flavour of garlic. I serve the salmon, garlic and broad beans with buerre blanc which is a simple emulsion of white wine, vinegar and butter.

To make the beurre blanc:

Combine the white wine, shallot and vinegar in a saucepan and reduce to a glaze. Do not allow to colour. Before the liquid evaporates, add the cream and remove the pan from the heat. Whisk in the diced butter, piece by piece until all the butter has melted and emulsified with the wine and vinegar reduction.

Strain through a fine sieve and add the finely chopped chives. Season with salt and pepper and keep warm.

Blanch the broad beans in a saucepan of boiling water for 30 seconds, then refresh immediately in a bowl of ice cold water and remove the skins.

Cook the salmon skin-side down in 2 tbsp olive oil in a non-stick frying pan for 2–3 minutes, or until the skin is crispy. Turn the salmon over and cook for a further 2 minutes then remove from the pan and set aside. Keep warm until ready to serve.

Sauté the garlic in remaining 2 tbsp olive oil in another frying pan. Add the broad beans with the water and cook for 1–2 minutes. Add the butter and season with salt and pepper.

Place the broad beans in the centre of 4 large serving plates, place the salmon on top, drizzle the beurre blanc around the outside of the plates and serve.

For the buerre blanc

200 ml/7 fl oz white wine

1 large shallot, peeled and finely sliced

100 ml/3½ fl oz white wine vinegar

2 tbsp double cream

100 g/3½ oz butter, diced and chilled

2 tsp fresh chives, finely chopped

salt and freshly ground black pepper

180 g/6½ oz broad beans, fresh (after their removal from pod)

4 x 160 g/5½ oz portion salmon fillet, skin-on

4 tbsp olive oil

1 garlic clove, peeled and crushed

100 ml/3½ fl oz water

25 g/1 oz butter

serves 4 as a main course

CRISPY PORK BELLY WITH CONFIT OF GARLIC AND A HONEY GLAZE

For the honey glaze
200 ml/7 fl oz honey
50 ml/2 fl oz dark soy sauce
1 tsp five-spice powder
1 tsp ground ginger
4 star anise
For the confit garlic
250 g/8 oz duck fat
12 garlic cloves, unpeeled
4 fresh thyme sprigs
2 bay leaves

50 ml/2 fl oz extra virgin olive oil
2 carrots, diced
2 celery sticks, diced
white of ½ leek
2 garlic cloves, crushed
3 plum tomatoes, de-seeded, diced
250 ml/8 fl oz white wine
1.2 litres/2 pints chicken stock
1.25–1.75 kg/2½–3½ lb pork belly
2 tsp olive oil
150 g/5 oz baby spinach
25 g/1 oz butter
2 fresh thyme sprigs

serves 6–8 as a main course

Pork belly is one of the tastiest joints of pork and the best thing of all is it is also one of the cheapest. It takes quite a while to cook but is very easy. Because of the high fat content, pork belly is rich and succulent and definitely something for a special occasion.

For the honey glaze:
Preheat oven to 140°C/275°F/Gas Mark 1. Combine all the ingredients for the honey glaze in a small saucepan and cook over a low heat for 5–7 minutes. Strain and reserve the star anise for the garnish.

For the garlic confit:
Heat the duck fat in a small saucepan over a low heat until it is hot to touch. Add the garlic, thyme and bay leaves and cook over a very low heat for about 15–20 minutes, or until the garlic is tender. Remove the pan from the heat, leave to cool and set aside until required.

Heat a large saucepan, add the olive oil and sweat the vegetables for 5 minutes. Add the wine and cook for a further 2 minutes. Add the chicken stock and herbs and bring to a simmer.

Place the pork belly in a large heavy-based casserole dish and pour over the hot chicken stock and vegetables. Cover with a lid and cook in the hot oven for about 2–3 hours, or until pork is tender.

Once the pork is ready, remove from the oven and place the pork on a baking tray with another tray on top and a weight (such as 2 cans of beans) to help weigh the pork down. Place in the refrigerator for about 3–4 hours, or preferably overnight.

Once the pork has been pressed, remove the trays and trim the pork into portions 15 cm/ 6 inches long and about 5 cm/2 inches wide.

Preheat oven to 180°C/350°F/Gas mark 4. Place the pork belly skin-side down in a non-stick cold frying pan with olive oil and begin to crisp the skin over a low–medium heat for about 1 minute, spooning half of the honey glaze over the pork.

Transfer the pork to the hot oven and colour on all sides. Spoon over the rest of the honey glaze while keeping a close eye that the pork does not burn.

Meanwhile, cook the spinach in the butter for 1 minute and set aside.

Once the pork is coloured and crispy, remove from the oven, slice and transfer to a serving plate. Garnish with the reserved star anise and thyme sprigs and serve with the garlic confit and spinach.

DEEP-FRIED COURGETTE FLOWERS
STUFFED WITH TALEGGIO AND BASIL

● ● ○

Everybody loved the classic dish deep-fried camembert and cranberry sauce. The reason this dish works so well is the same reason that the old one did – it's the combination of melted cheese with a sweet yet sharp jam sauce.

Combine the blackberries, balsamic vinegar and sugar in a medium sized hot saucepan and cook for 10–15 minutes. Remove the pan from the heat and push the mixture through a fine sieve. Reserve juice and discard the pulp.

Heat the oil for deep-frying in a deep saucepan to 160°C/325°F or until a cube of bread browns in 30 seconds.

To make the batter: Place the flour in a large mixing bowl and gradually pour in the water, mixing constantly with your fingertips. It doesn't matter if the batter has a few lumps. Set aside until required.

Cut the Taleggio into 12 even-sized pieces and wrap each one in a basil leaf. Place one piece of cheese into each courgette flower and twist at the top.

Dust the courgette flowers in a little flour and dip into the batter mixture. Your oil should now be hot so deep-fry the flowers for 1½–2½ minutes until light golden. Leave to drain on kitchen paper.

Season with salt and pepper and serve with a drizzle of the blackberry and balsamic reduction.

2 punnets blackberries
100 ml/3½ fl oz balsamic vinegar
25 g/1 oz caster sugar
200 g/7 oz plain flour, plus extra
   for dusting
150 ml/5 fl oz ice cold water
180 g/6½ oz Taleggio cheese
12 fresh basil leaves
12 courgette flowers
2 litres/3 pints vegetable oil,
   for frying
salt and freshly ground
   black pepper

serves 4 as a starter

● ● ●　STEAMED SNAPPER WITH CLAMS, COURGETTES AND THEIR FLOWERS

This dish is lovely and light, perfectly healthy and ideal for a summer's day. If you have the stock already on hand the snapper can be cooked within minutes. If you can't buy snapper, a great alternative would be bream or sea bass.

For the stock

300 g/11 oz white fish bones, cleaned

bones of 2 snapper, eyes and gills removed

200 ml/7 fl oz white wine

1 shallot, peeled and coarsely chopped

the white of 1 leek

1 celery rib, coarsely chopped

1 bay leaf

1 fresh thyme

¼ bunch of fresh parsley stalks

2 litres/3½ pints water

2 x 600 g/1¼ lb snapper fillets

butter, for greasing

20 fresh clams

6 baby courgettes

6 courgette flowers, with stem

To garnish

olive oil

fresh chervil and dill sprigs

serves 4 as a main course

To make the stock:

Rinse the fish bones under cold running water and place in a large stockpot or saucepan. Place over a medium heat and add the white wine, vegetables, herbs and water. Bring slowly to a simmer, constantly skimming the stock with a slotted spoon. Once it has reached a gentle simmer, leave to simmer for 20 minutes. Remove the stockpot from the heat and leave to stand for 5 minutes.

Carefully ladle the stock from the top of the pot into another pot passing the stock through a muslin cloth. Reduce the stock by a third.

Bring 400 ml/14 fl oz of the fish stock to the boil in the base of a double saucepan.

Place the snapper fillets on some lightly greased greaseproof paper then arrange in a steamer, cover with the lid and place on top of the saucepan.

After 1 minute, place the clams and courgettes in the stock and cook for a further 1–2 minutes. The fish is cooked when a cocktail stick is inserted into the largest point of the fish without any resistance. The clams are cooked when they are open.

Remove the pan from the heat and take the clams and courgettes out of the liquid. Drop ribbons of courgette flowers into the hot stock and leave for 30 seconds.

Place the courgettes in the centre of a large bowl and place the snapper on top. Ladle the stock over the snapper and place the clams around it with the courgette flowers. Garnish the stock with a little olive oil, and sprigs of chervil and dill, and serve.

SCALLOPS

There are hundreds of species of scallops, fresh and salt water. In the following recipes I have used Scottish sea scallops which I consider to be the best.

Scallops live in or around sandy or weedy beds. The best way to collect these jewels of the sea is to dive and hand-collect them. Good fisherman will move from one area to the next so as not to over-fish a particular area. The other method of collection is to dredge for them. I personally think that this should be outlawed and would never cook a dredged scallop for two reasons: firstly when the nets are dredged over the ocean bed you completely over-fish a particular area, secondly the scallops usually die in the net so they tend to fill with sand. Scallops take very little cooking and can even be served raw. Try to buy them still in their shell. Ask your fishmonger for hand-dived scallops and eat them as fresh as possible.

Good levels of omega-3 fatty acids. High in protein, vitamin B, magnesium and potassium.

BBQ SCALLOPS IN THE HALF SHELL WITH CITRUS FRUITS AND WHITE WINE

50 ml/2 fl oz citrus juice
100 ml/3½ fl oz white wine
150 ml/5 fl oz extra virgin
  olive oil
1 tbsp fresh flat-leaf parsley,
  coarsely chopped
12 cleaned scallops with roe in
  the half shell
2 oranges, 2 lemons and
  2 grapefruit, segmented

serves 4 as a starter

It's hard to believe that a recipe with only three steps can taste so divine. But it does! What better way to spend a summer's day than standing outside in the sun with a beer in your hand looking down at a hot barbecue covered in scallops in their half shell.

Light a barbecue. Whisk the citrus juice, white wine and olive oil together in a bowl. Add the parsley and mix into the dressing. Spoon the citrus juice dressing over the scallops and place on a red hot barbecue for 3–5 minutes.

Cut each of the fruit segments into 5 pieces, spoon over the scallops and serve.

ROASTED SEA SCALLOP WRAPPED IN PANCETTA WITH TOMATO AND GREMOLATA

● ● ○

The smoky flavour of the pancetta works beautifully with the delicate flavour of the sea scallops. It is important to make sure that the pancetta is sliced very thinly so not to overpower the flavour of the scallops.

To make the gremolata

Mix the parsley, garlic and the zest and juice of the oranges, lime and 1 of the lemons together in a small bowl. Season with salt and pepper, add the olive oil and set the gremolata aside until ready to serve.

Preheat oven to 180°C/350°F/Gas Mark 4. Trim the pancetta to 1 cm/½ inch in width and 10 cm/4 inches in length then place 2 strips of pancetta across each other flat on a baking tray to make a cross. Place a scallop large-side down in the centre of the cross and wrap the pancetta around the scallop. Repeat until all the scallops are used.

Heat a large non-stick frying pan. Place the scallops flat-side down for 30 seconds until they begin to change colour (in batches if necessary). Transfer the pan to the oven for 1 minute, then turn them over and cook for a further 1 minute. Remove from the oven.

Place the diced tomatoes, the juice of 1 lemon and the olive oil in a small pan and warm gently.

To serve, place the tomatoes in the centre of 4 serving plates. Place the scallops on top and lay a few baby salad leaves in the centre of the scallops. Drizzle a little of the dressing used to warm the tomatoes over the leaves and spoon the gremolata around the plates.

For the gremolata

4 tbsp fresh flat-leaf parsley, coarsely chopped
2 garlic cloves, peeled and crushed
zest and juice of 2 oranges
zest and juice of 1 lime
juice of 1 lemon
salt and freshly ground black pepper
100 ml/3½ fl oz extra virgin olive oil

24 thin slices of pancetta
12 sea scallops
4 tomatoes, blanched, peeled, de-seeded and diced
juice of 1 lemon
2 tbsp olive oil
baby salad leaves, to serve

serves 4 as a starter

● ● ●

TARTARE OF HAND-DIVED SEA SCALLOPS WITH TOMATO ESSENCE AND OSCIETRE CAVIAR

This dish is actually very easy to make, however, it can be slightly time consuming and expensive. If you can't purchase the caviar, just leave it out – the dish will still work. The tomato essence can also be served as a starter or palate cleanser.

For the tomato essence

2 beef tomatoes, coarsely chopped

5 plum tomatoes, coarsely chopped

½ cucumber, peeled, de-seeded
  and coarsely chopped

2 tsp Maldon sea salt

¼ bunch of fresh chives, coarsely
  chopped

¼ bunch of fresh basil leaves

¼ bunch of fresh tarragon leaves

¼ bunch of fresh chervil leaves

For the tartare

12 large sea scallops, finely diced

½ lime juice

2 tbsp cucumber, peeled,
  de-seeded and finely diced

25 fresh coriander leaves,
  finely sliced

salt and freshly ground
  black pepper

50 g/2 oz oscietre caviar

extra virgin olive oil to drizzle

few fresh chervil leaves

serves 4 as a starter

For the tomato essence:

Place all the ingredients for the tomato essence in a food processor and pulse for 30 seconds. Strain through a fine sieve lined with muslin into a bowl. Allow the tomato essence to drip through the muslin. This may take 2 hours.

Cover the strained tomato essence with cling-film and chill in the refrigerator until required.

For the tartare:

Combine the diced scallops, lime juice, cucumber and coriander in a small bowl and season with salt and pepper.

When ready to serve, place a small round biscuit cutter on each serving plate and pack the scallop mixture into it. Remove the cutter. Place the caviar on top of the scallop mixture and slowly pour the chilled tomato essence around the scallops.

Drizzle droplets of olive oil around the edge of the tomato essence, sprinkle a few chervil leaves over the tartare and serve.

VEAL

Veal is the meat from a cow less than a year old. Milk-fed veal (a calf yet to be weaned) is the best quality. When choosing meat it should be a light pink colour which will mean that it is very tender. When a calf begins to eat grass its flesh starts to change colour to a deeper red and the meat becomes tougher.

The thing to remember about veal is it is a very young and lean meat, so I always say you need to treat it a little more delicately. Cook it on a slightly lower temperatue and never cook it past medium.

Excellent source of vitamin B3 (niacin) and a good source of iron, protein, zinc and selenium, thiamin, vitamins B2 (riboflavin), B12 and vitamin C.

CHARGRILLED VEAL CHOP WITH SEMI-DRIED TOMATOES AND WATERCRESS

The peppery flavour of the watercress and the sweetness of the tomato balance beautifully next to the delicate flavour of the veal. If you find it hard to source such a grand piece of meat, you may like to opt for a piece of veal loin instead.

Preheat oven to 120°C/250°F/Gas Mark ½. Cut the tomatoes in half lengthways and place on a baking tray. Place a sprig of thyme, a slice of garlic and a pinch of salt on each tomato half and drizzle with olive oil. Place in the oven for 1½ hours.

Preheat a griddle pan or light a barbecue. Season the veal chops with salt and pepper then place on the griddle pan or on the barbecue and leave to chargrill for 1–2 minutes until coloured. Turn the veal over and cook for a further 2–3 minutes.

Place the semi-dried tomatoes and veal chops on 4 serving plates, garnish with some watercress, drizzle with olive oil and serve.

6 plum tomatoes
12 fresh thyme sprigs
2 garlic cloves, peeled and
   finely sliced
pinch of sea salt
100 ml/3½ fl oz extra virgin
   olive oil
4 veal chops,
   approx 350 g/11½ oz each
salt and freshly ground black
   pepper
watercress sprigs, to garnish

serves 4 as a main course

PARMESAN CRUSTED VEAL ESCALOPE WITH ROASTED RED PEPPERS

● ● ○

Veal is ideal to serve in breadcrumbs and pan fry as it is so tender. The Parmesan cheese crust gives this a real Mediterranean flavour that is so tasty and works perfectly with the sweetness of the red peppers.

To roast the red peppers:

Preheat oven to 220°C/425°F/Gas Mark 7. Heat a baking tray. Add the red peppers and drizzle olive oil. Place in the hot oven for 15–20 minutes, turning them every 5 minutes.

Remove the peppers from the oven and place in a large bowl. Cover with clingfilm and leave to stand for about 20 minutes. As soon as the peppers are cool enough to handle, carefully remove the skin and seeds and cut the flesh into strips.

Mix the pepper strips with some extra virgin olive oil and parsley in a pan and warm gently while cooking the veal.

For the veal:

Mix the breadcrumbs and Parmesan cheese together in a small bowl. Create the egg wash by mixing the broken eggs and milk with a fork. Dip the veal escalopes into the flour, then into the egg-and-milk wash and finally into the breadcrumbs to coat, making sure they are pressed firmly into the veal.

Heat the butter and 2 tsp olive oil in a large non-stick frying pan. Add the veal escalopes (in batches if necessary) and cook over a medium heat for 2–3 minutes until golden brown. Turn the veal over and cook until golden brown.

Add the capers, lemon and parsley to the pan and stir, then remove the veal and leave to drain on kitchen paper.

Place a pile of the peppers on each of 4 serving plates and lay the veal on top. Drizzle a little of the capers and butter around the plates then garnish with anchovies and serve.

4 red peppers
50 ml/2 fl oz olive oil
100 ml/3½ fl oz extra virgin olive oil
80 g/3¼ oz fresh breadcrumbs
100 g/3½ oz Parmesan cheese
4 x 100 g/3½ oz veal escalopes
200 g/7 oz plain flour
3 eggs
1 tbsp milk
2 tbsp butter
2 tsp olive oil
50 g/2 oz extra fine capers
1 lemon, segmented
1 tbsp fresh parsley, coarsely chopped
8 marinated anchovy fillets, to garnish

serves 4 as a main course

● ● ●

POACHED VEAL FILLET WITH
BABY SPINACH AND GIROLES

For the poaching liquid

1 litre/1¾ pints chicken stock

½ celery rib, coarsely chopped

½ shallot, peeled and coarsely
chopped

½ carrot, peeled and coarsely
chopped

2 garlic cloves, peeled and
cut in half

1 bay leaf

1 fresh thyme sprig

4 x 180 g/6½ oz veal fillets

200 g/7 oz giroles

1 shallot, peeled and finely diced

salt and freshly ground black
pepper

100 g/3½ oz baby spinach,
washed with stalks removed

serves 4 as a main course

In this recipe the poaching liquid becomes the sauce, making it a very light summery dish. Personally, I don't think this dish is adventurous at all but I know that some people are scared of poaching meats, so give this a go and let me prove how simple it can be!

Place all the ingredients for the poaching liquid in a large saucepan and bring to a simmer.

Heat a medium frying pan and seal the veal fillets on all sides until golden brown. Place the veal into the poaching liquid and poach for about 8–10 minutes then remove and leave to rest for 4 minutes before carving into thin slices.

Meanwhile, add the giroles, shallot and salt and pepper to the frying pan and sauté for 2–3 minutes. When the girolles are cooked, remove from the pan and keep warm. Place the same pan back on the heat and add the spinach and leave to wilt.

Squeeze the excess moisture from the spinach with the back of a fork and place in the centre of each of 4 serving plates and scatter the giroles around the outside of the plates. Place slices of veal on the plates, spoon a little of the poaching liquid over the meat to act as sauce, and serve.

RASPBERRIES

When I was young I would go berry picking with my mum and brother. We used to get in such a mess but the rewards were great. Raspberries first appear around June and their season lasts about 4–5 months.

Raspberries, like any other fruit, should only be eaten when perfectly ripe. The berries should be soft and a vibrant red colour. My tip is buy them when they are cheap and make things that will keep a while, such as jams, etc.

High in dietary fibre and vitamin C and manganese

RASPBERRY SORBET AND CHOCOLATE BONBONS

I used to serve these as petit fours in a Michelin-starred restaurant in London, however, I've also made them with a group of kids who not only loved making them but certainly enjoyed eating them, even if a few of our balls resembled marshmallows!

1 x 750 ml/1¼ pints raspberry sorbet
400 g/14 oz plain dark chocolate
100 g/3½ oz white chocolate

serves 4

Wrap a layer of clingfilm over a baking tray. Using a melon baller, scoop the raspberry sorbet into small balls and place on the baking tray. Do this as quickly as possible so the sorbet doesn't begin to melt. Leave the balls to set firmly in the freezer overnight.

Break the plain dark chocolate into small pieces in a small heatproof bowl. Set the bowl over a pan of simmering water and stir until melted and smooth.

Take the sorbet balls out of the freezer, push a cocktail stick in each ball and dip them into the melted chocolate. Do this in batches as the sorbet will melt if it sits out of the freezer for too long. Insert the coated balls into anything that will let them sit upright in the freezer, such as a piece of polystyrene. Once all the balls have been coated thoroughly in chocolate, place them back into the freezer until the chocolate has set, about 30 minutes.

Meanwhile, break the white chocolate up into small pieces and melt in the same way as the plain dark chocolate.

Remove the balls from the freezer and drizzle the melted white chocolate over the balls. Place them back into the freezer for 30 minutes. Once the white chocolate has set, place the balls on a plate and serve.

PASSION FRUIT AND RASPBERRY
CRÈME CARAMEL

I have always loved the combination of raspberries and passion fruit. This is a light dessert that shows off both fruits magnificently and, trust me, it tastes even better than it looks.

To make the caramel:

Preheat oven to 140°C/275°F/Gas Mark 1. Place the sugar in a medium saucepan over a low–medium heat and allow the sugar to melt. Once the sugar has melted it will begin to colour gradually. When the sugar becomes golden brown remove from the heat and add the passion fruit. Stir, then immediately pour the caramel evenly into the base of 4 ramekins. Leave to cool.

To make the crème

Warm the caster sugar, milk, cream and vanilla extract in a separate medium saucepan, stirring constantly, until the sugar dissolves. Remove the pan from the heat and leave to cool slightly, about 5 minutes.

Whisk the eggs and egg yolks together in a bowl using a small balloon whisk, add the eggs to the cooled milk and stir until combined. Strain the mixture and pour into the ramekins.

Place the ramekins in a bain-marie or a roasting tray half-filled with warm water and carefully place in the hot oven for 60 minutes.

To test whether the crème caramels are ready, push a small knife into the centre of one of the dishes and if the caramel rises out of the hole left by the knife, then they are ready.

Remove the crème caramels from the oven and allow to cool. Leave to set in the refrigerator overnight.

When serving the crème caramels run a knife around the inside of each ramekin and turn out onto individual serving plates. Decorate with fresh raspberries and serve.

For the caramel
200 g/7 oz caster sugar
5 passion fruit

For the crème
100 g/3½ oz caster sugar
250 ml/8 fl oz milk
250 ml/8 fl oz double cream
1 tsp vanilla extract
3 eggs
3 egg yolks
1 punnet raspberries

serves 4–6

● ● ● # RASPBERRY SOUFFLÉ
WITH RASPBERRY SAUCE

For the raspberry sauce
2 punnets raspberries
75 g/3 oz icing sugar
To line the dishes
50 g/2 oz butter, melted
100 g/3½ oz caster sugar
For the soufflé
½ jar raspberry jam, seedless
75 g/3 oz cornflour
50 ml/2 fl oz water
250 ml/8 fl oz egg whites
130 g/4¼ oz caster sugar
icing sugar, for dusting
4 raspberries, to decorate

serves 6

To be honest soufflés were invented as a way for chefs to use up excess egg whites. So many recipes call for egg yolks and I hate wasting food, so I just had to include a recipe to use up the egg whites. It's a light dessert and ideal to follow a large dinner.

To make the raspberry sauce:
Preheat oven to 190°C/375°F/Gas Mark 5. Place the raspberries and icing sugar in a blender and purée until smooth. Push the purée through a fine sieve, discarding the seeds and reserving the sauce for later.

To make the soufflé base:
Place the raspberry jam in a small saucepan over a medium heat and leave until the jam begins to boil.

Combine the cornflour and water in a small bowl then slowly add the mixture to the raspberry jam, stirring constantly. Once the jam resembles a thick paste, remove from the heat and leave to cool.

To line the soufflé dishes:
Brush the melted butter carefully around the inside of 6 individual soufflé dishes then sprinkle the inside of the dishes with caster sugar, discarding any excess sugar. Place the dishes in the freezer for 5 minutes then repeat the process, making sure that the first coating of sugar is not scraped away. Using a pastry brush, paint 6 stripes of the raspberry sauce onto the inside of the soufflé dishes, being careful not to disturb any sugar. Return the soufflé dishes to the freezer.

Using an electric whisk on high speed, whisk the egg whites and 2 tbsp of the caster sugar together in a large mixing bowl until the egg whites begin to thicken. Add the rest of the sugar and continue whisking on high speed until the egg whites resemble stiff peaks.

Mix the raspberry purée thoroughly with one-third of the egg whites then gently fold in the remainder of the egg whites to create a light mixture. Remove the soufflé dishes from the freezer and fill them to the top with the soufflé mixture. Using a palette knife, ensure the soufflé dishes are full then evenly level the top.

Place the dishes immediately in the hot oven for 10–13 minutes until the souffles have risen to nearly double the size of the dish. Dust with icing sugar, decorate with a raspberry and serve immediately with the raspberry sauce.

AUTUMN

When the early autumn approaches the winds start to pick up and the leaves begin to change colour, as does our appetite. We are moving towards colder weather and heartier foods. As the nights start to get shorter we feel like staying in and enjoying nourishing food in the warmth of our homes. When I lived in Australia I would always get a little depressed in autumn – the holidays were over, the good weather disappearing and the parties thin on the ground. However,

when I first arrived in London I was introduced to the autumn game season and now every year I get very excited awaiting the opening of the pheasant season. Then the first partridges, which are followed closely by grouse. I like the fact that they all come at slightly different times as it allows you to concentrate on one ingredient at a time.

Meats like rabbit and hare are great this time of year and I think they suit the weather down to the ground. Even if you are not a game lover, autumn can still be a season for you. It's a great time to have the family around for a roast. Some root vegetables are really starting to come into their own – use parsnips and beetroots as often as you can. Apples are also great, so it's all about apple tarts, puddings and pies.

Autumn should be about comfort food: light some candles, open a nice bottle of red wine or two and relax.

PUMPKIN

We use pumpkin oil, pumpkin seeds, carved pumpkins for Halloween and that's all before we even turn on the oven. The beauty of this big variety of squash is they last for a long time so you can still be enjoying them into winter.

Pumpkin is quite often used as a substitute to a potato, and why not? However they are very different and have a high water content (90%). This means that you need to cook pumpkin for a long time to cook out some of the liquid and get a good intensive flavour.

Low in fat, cholesterol and salt as well as being high in fibre, iron and vitamins A and C.

PUMPKIN AND NUTMEG PURÉE

It's as though pumpkin and nutmeg were put on this earth to be used together. This is a great side dish to have on the table when you're serving a large number of people and it's particularly good with roasted meats.

Melt the butter in a large saucepan. Add the shallots and garlic and sweat over a low heat until soft, but not coloured. Add the pumpkin and some freshly grated nutmeg then cover with a lid and cook over a medium heat for 20 minutes, stirring frequently.

Remove the lid and continue cooking until all the liquid has evaporated. Transfer to a blender and process until smooth.

Transfer the purée to a serving dish, garnish with more freshly grated nutmeg and serve hot.

100 g/3½ oz butter
3 shallots, thinly sliced
3 garlic cloves, peeled and sliced
2 kg/4½ lb pumpkin, peeled and diced
¼ nutmeg, grated

serves 4–6 as a side dish

ROAST LOIN OF FREE-RANGE PORK WITH ROAST PUMPKIN

There is nothing better than a good piece of roast pork with yummy crackling. Make sure that the piece of pork is free-range, and if possible, organic. Trust me, you will taste the difference.

Preheat oven to 220°C/425°F/Gas Mark 7. Score the loin of pork with a very sharp knife and rub with the salt and sugar. Place on a rack in a roasting tray and roast in the oven for 20 minutes with the olive oil. Reduce oven temperature to 180°C/350°F/Gas Mark 4 and cook for a further 50 minutes.

Preheat a separate large oven tray. Pour some oil on the tray and add the pumpkin. Make sure that there is not too much pumpkin on one tray so the pumpkin does not go soggy.

Sprinkle the pumpkin with marjoram leaves and roast in the oven for the last 30 minutes of the pork's cooking time. Keep turning the pumpkin over to make sure it cooks evenly. Drizzle the pumpkin with maple syrup and return to the oven to keep warm until ready to serve.

Once the pork is cooked and skin is nice and crispy, remove from the oven and leave to rest for 20 minutes. Carve the pork and serve with the roast pumpkin.

1.5 kg/3¼ lb loin of pork
100 g/3½ oz Maldon sea salt
25 g/1 oz caster sugar
2 tbsp olive oil
1.5 kg/3¼ lb pumpkin, peeled
   and cut into chunks
1 tbsp fresh marjoram leaves
50 ml/2 fl oz maple syrup

serves 6 as a main course

● ● ●

HOMEMADE RAVIOLI OF PUMPKIN AND PARMESAN WITH PINE KERNELS

For the ravioli filling

300 g/11 oz pumpkin purée (see recipe on page 85)

2 tbsp olive oil

200 g/7 oz pumpkin, peeled and diced into 1-cm/½-inch cubes

1 tsp fresh tarragon, finely chopped

120 g/4¼ oz freshly grated Parmesan cheese

salt and freshly ground black pepper

For the pasta dough

550 g/1⅓ lb Italian "OO" flour, plus extra for dusting

6 egg yolks

4 whole eggs

2 tbsp extra virgin olive oil

120 g/4¼ oz butter

25 sage leaves

juice of 2 lemons

100 g/3½ oz pine kernels

40 g/1½ oz Parmesan shavings

serves 4–6 as a starter or main course

There's no two ways about it, the first time you make ravioli, it will be a little difficult. The beauty of it is, after only a little practice of handling the pasta dough you will enjoy it so much, you may even become obsessed.

To make the ravioli filling:

Place the pumpkin purée in a small saucepan and leave over a medium heat for 7–8 minutes, stirring constantly and making sure it doesn't catch. Leave to cool.

Heat a little olive oil in a small non-stick frying pan and cook the diced pumpkin for about 8–10 minutes until it turns golden brown. Leave to cool.

Mix the cooled purée, diced pumpkin, tarragon and Parmesan together and season with salt and pepper to taste. Set aside.

To make the pasta dough:

Using your hands combine the flour, egg yolks, egg and extra virgin olive oil in a large mixing bowl. Knead the mixture until the dough resembles a smooth paste-like texture, then cover the dough in clingfilm and leave to rest in the refrigerator for 1 hour.

Using a pasta machine, roll the dough until it is 1–2 mm/¹⁄₁₆ inch thick.

Lightly dust a work surface with flour and place the pasta sheets on the work surface. Cut pieces of pasta into 8 cm/3 inch squares. Place 2–3 tsp of pumpkin mixture in the centre of one pasta square and brush the edge of the pasta sheet with a little water. Place the second pasta sheet on top of the pumpkin mixture and press down gently around the filling to seal and expel any air. Trim the ravioli, if necessary, and drop into a large saucepan of boiling salted water and cook for 5–6 minutes or until they rise to the surface.

Place a large frying pan over a high heat and when hot, add the butter and leave until melted and a light brown colour. Add the sage leaves and lemon juice and remove the pan from the heat.

Carefully drain the ravioli with a slotted spoon and place 3 on each serving plate. Spoon the brown butter and sage mix over the ravioli and garnish with pine kernels and Parmesan shavings.

CRAB

To me, crabs are a bit like lobster – an absolute delicacy. There are hundreds of species of crab the world over, but I find the Cornish crab is as good as any I have ever tasted. In fact crab would have to be my favourite food from the sea. I know that things can get a little bit messy when you are cleaning them up and picking the meat from them, however the rewards far outweigh the effort. White crab meat is found in the claws, legs and body and the brown meat is found in the head (top of the shell).

Crab is low in fat and high in protein and omega-3 fatty acids (good for cardiovascular health)

WHOLE CRACKED CRAB
WITH HOME-MADE MAYONNAISE

This is the ultimate way to share a dish with those with which you are close. Although it can get a little messy it makes for half the fun. So take your time and enjoy the sweet taste of these beautiful crabs. I think it's even worth popping a nice bottle of bubbly!

To make the mayonnaise: Place the egg yolks, mustard and vinegar in a food processor and process briefly on high speed until pale and creamy. With the motor still running, through the feeder tube slowly add the vegetable oil in a constant drizzle until the mayonnaise begins to thicken. Once most of the oil is incorporated into the egg yolk add a little warm water to thin the mixture. Continue adding the oil and warm water until the desired consistency is achieved, then season with salt and pepper and leave to chill in a covered bowl until required.

To cook the crab: If the crab is bought alive, the most humane way to kill it is to lay it on its back and use a kitchen steel or sharp knife to penetrate the shell underneath the tail by pushing the instrument as quickly as possible (ideally in one move) through the crab.

Place all the vegetables, peppercorns, bay leaves and thyme in a large saucepan and bring to the boil. Once water is boiling, add the whole crab and cook for 15–18 minutes. Remove crab and leave to cool in the refrigerator for about 1 hour.

Crack the crab claws with a hammer or nut-crackers and serve chilled with crusty bread and home-made mayonnaise.

For the mayonnaise
2 egg yolks
2 tsp Dijon mustard
2 tsp white wine vinegar
200 ml/7 fl oz vegetable oil
2 tbsp warm water

1 x 2–3 kg/4½–6½ lb fresh crab
1 leek, coarsely chopped
1 celery stick, coarsely chopped
1 onion, coarsely chopped
10 white peppercorns
2 bay leaves
1 fresh thyme sprig
crusty bread, to serve

serves 4–6 as a main course

● ● ○

FRESH ORECCHIETTE
WITH CRAB AND CHILLI

150 g/5 oz crabmeat, picked

250 g/9 oz dried orecchiette
pasta

salt and cracked black pepper

2 tbsp olive oil

2 shallots, peeled and finely
chopped

2 garlic cloves, peeled and
crushed

2 fresh chillies, finely chopped

150 ml/5 fl oz dry white wine

12 cocktail crab claws, cooked

100 ml/3½ fl oz extra virgin
olive oil

2 tbsp fresh flat-leaf parsley,
coarsely chopped

serves 4 as a starter or
main course

Crab and chilli have been served all over Italy with hundreds of variations for centuries. This is mine. It's quick, simple and if you get your hands on a good fresh crab, will bring a smile to your face..

If you are buying crabs uncooked, cook them according to the method used on page 91.

Cook the orecchiette in a large saucepan of salted boiling water for 10–12 minutes, or until al dente (tender but firm to the bite).

Meanwhile, sweat the shallots, garlic and chilli with 2 tbsp of olive oil in a separate large high-sided pan until soft but not coloured. Add the white wine, crabmeat and claws then season with salt and pepper.

Remove the pan from the heat and add the extra virgin olive oil and parsley, stirring constantly.

Drain the cooked pasta and add it to the crab mixture. Toss together and serve immediately in 4 warmed pasta bowls.

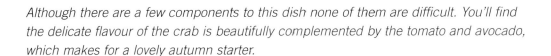

CRAB, CARROT AND CELERIAC SALAD
WITH AVOCADO CREAM AND GAZPACHO

Although there are a few components to this dish none of them are difficult. You'll find the delicate flavour of the crab is beautifully complemented by the tomato and avocado, which makes for a lovely autumn starter.

For the gazpacho:

Combine all the ingredients together except the olive oil in a bowl then leave to stand at room temperature for 12 hours.

Tranfer the mixture to a blender and process until smooth. Slowly add the olive oil, to taste. Adjust the seasoning, cover with clingfilm and leave to chill in the refrigerator until required.

For the avocado cream:

Place all the ingredients in a food processor and process until smooth. Season to taste.

Transfer to a bowl, cover with clingfilm and place in the refrigerator until required.

For the crab salad:

Blanch the carrot and celeriac in a saucepan of boiling water until tender, about 2–4 minutes.

Refresh in cold water and placing them in a cloth, squeeze out the excess water before mixing with the crab, mayonnaise and lemon juice. Season to taste.

Place a round biscuit cutter, 3 cm/1¼ inches in diameter, into the centre of a large serving plate. Fill the cutter with the crab salad and remove the cutter.

Using 2 spoons, transfer a small amount of the avocado cream from one to the other, making nice egg-shaped quenelles. Place a quenelle of avocado cream on top of the crab salad, pour gazpacho around the salad to fill the plate and serve.

or the gazpacho

175 g/6 oz cucumber, peeled, diced

250 g/9 oz tomato, diced

25 g/1 oz onion, diced

75 g/3 oz green pepper, diced

½ garlic clove, roughly chopped

½ tsp ground cumin

500 ml/16 fl oz chicken stock

2.5 tsp red wine vinegar

salt and pepper, to taste

12.5 ml olive oil

175 ml/6 fl oz tomato juice

½ fresh hot red chilli, finely chopped

25 g/1 oz tomato purée

2 slices white bread, without crusts

For the avocado cream

2 avocados

squeeze of lemon juice

salt

2 tsp crème fraîche (or sour cream)

For the crab salad

½ carrot, peeled and cut into matchsticks

¼ celeriac, peeled and cut into matchsticks

400 g/14 oz picked crabmeat

50 g/2 oz home-made mayonnaise (see page 91)

juice of 1 lemon

serves 4 as a starter

PROSCIUTTO

PProsciutto as a direct translation is ham. *Prosciutto crudo* in Italian refers to cured or salted, aged, air-dried ham which is what I shall focus on here. The process of making prosciutto involves curing or salting a leg of pork for between 5–13 days. The ham is then hung in non-refrigerated storage units (the air flow is particularly important) and aged for up to 18 months. While *Proscuitto di Parma*, or Parma ham, may be the most famous of all, there are endless varieties and it is made all over Europe. Some of the better known varieties include: Italy – *Prosciutto di San Danielle*, *di Norica*, *di Parma*; France – *jambon de bayonne*; Spain – *Iberico* and *Serrano*; Germany – *Schinken*.

The way you have most probably eaten prosciutto is thinly sliced with some fresh fruit, like melon or figs, and let's face it, it's not a bad way to spend an afternoon. What I also like doing is cooking with prosciutto as I have done in the following recipes. I love the strong salty taste mixed with other wonderful autumn ingredients.

Prosciutto is very high in protein, iron and vitamin B.

PROSCIUTTO WITH FIGS AND BALSAMIC VINEGAR

12 thin slices of prosciutto
3 figs, cut into quarters
150 ml/5 fl oz balsamic vinegar
breadsticks, to serve

Serves 4 as a starter

When the figs are ripe and the prosciutto is finely sliced, I think it's hard to find a better autumn dish. If your budget allows it, try to buy a balsamic vinegar that's been aged with no added sugar; the older, the better.

Reduce the balsamic vinegar to a glaze in a small saucepan. Place the slices of prosciutto on a large serving plate, place figs in the centre and drizzle a little balsamic vinegar around the prosciutto. Serve with breadsticks.

WARM SALAD OF CRISPY PROSCIUTTO, BABY BEETS AND FIELD MUSHROOMS

I still love eating salads even during colder weather. This is an example of a salad that can be served warm with a combination of hearty ingredients that taste great.

Preheat oven to 180°C/350°F/Gas Mark 4. Lay the baby beetroot on a large roasting tray. Drizzle with olive oil and season with salt and pepper. Place in the hot oven for 20–25 minutes, or until the beetroot is tender. Remove from the oven and keep warm.

Place the prosciutto in a large non-stick frying pan and allow it to go crispy. Once crispy, turn the prosciutto over and remove from the pan. Leave to cool until required. Using the same pan, add the mushrooms, season and cook in the excess fat from the prosciutto

for 2–3 minutes (you may need a little extra butter).

Remove the mushrooms from the pan set aside. In the same pan, but not on the heat, combine the sherry vinegar and the extra virgin olive oil with a whisk for the dressing.

Mix the baby beetroot, salad leaves and mushrooms together in a large bowl with the dressing. Place the salad leaves on each of 4 serving plates, then place the crispy prosciutto on top and serve.

2 bunches baby beetroot
100 ml/3½ fl oz extra virgin olive
    oil, plus extra for drizzling
salt and freshly ground
    black pepper
4 slices prosciutto
4 large mushrooms
100 ml/3½ fl oz sherry vinegar
1 shallot, finely diced
80 g/3 ¼ oz mixed salad leaves

serves 4 as a starter

GUINEA FOWL WRAPPED IN PROSCIUTTO WITH ROMANESCO BROCCOLI

r the sauce

2 tbsp vegetable oil

1 kg/2¼ lb chicken wings

2 shallots, peeled and finely sliced

½ bunch of fresh rosemary

75 ml/2½ fl oz Maderia

75 ml/2½ fl oz white wine

1.5 litres/2½ pints chicken stock

2 bay leaves

4 guinea fowl suprêmes, skin
   removed

8 sage leaves

8 large thin slices prosciutto

2 Romanesco broccoli, trimmed
   into florets

3 garlic cloves, peeled and sliced
   thinly on a Japanese mandolin

salt and freshly ground black pepper

40 g/1½ oz butter

100 ml/3½ fl oz white wine

serves 4 as a main course

The easiest way to describe guinea fowl is to compare it to chicken. It has less meat and more flavour. But if you can't get your hands on it, chicken is an obvious substitute. Romanesco broccoli is only found in autumn but tastes great.

For the sauce:

Heat the oil in a large high-sided pan, preheated for 4-5 minutes. Add the chicken wings and brown over a high heat until coloured. Pour off the excess oil and add the shallots, the bunch of rosemary and the bay leaves. Cook for 2–3 minutes.

Deglaze the pan with the Madeira and white wine, then reduce the liquor to half. Add the stock and bring to a near simmer, then simmer for 1 hour, skimming constantly with a ladle. Strain the sauce into a clean pan, return to the heat, bring back to the boil and skim until the consistency is that of cream.

Preheat oven to 180°C/350°F/Gas Mark 4. Wrap each guinea fowl suprême with 2 sage leaves and 2 slices of prosciutto.

Place the guinea fowl suprêmes, skin-side-down in a large non-stick frying pan and cook for 1–2 minutes until the prosciutto is golden. Turn the guinea fowl over, transfer to a baking tray and place in the hot oven for 4–5 minutes.

Remove the guinea fowl from the oven and leave to rest for 3 minutes.

Meanwhile, blanch the broccoli in a saucepan of salted boiling water for 3–5 minutes or until tender, then strain.

In the same pan used for cooking the guinea fowl, add the garlic and strained broccoli, then season with salt and pepper and add the white wine and butter. Toss together for 1 minute, then remove the broccoli and place on individual serving plates.

Slice the guinea fowl and serve around the broccoli. Drizzle the sauce over and serve.

GAME BIRDS

Both the UK and mainland Europe have a huge tradition of hunting wild birds. The season is different for each bird with most lasting two or three months over autumn and winter. After the birds are shot they need to age to improve flavour and tenderness. It is of personal preference as to how long the birds are hung – some prefer to eat the bird "high" after the meat has aged for a longer period of time. The usual period for hanging a pheasant for example is 3–7 days (or 5+ days for a high meat).

It should be noted that if you buy your bird from a reputable butcher you will not need to age the bird any further. All game birds should be cooked medium to medium-rare.

● ○ ○   ## ROAST WILD DUCK WITH CARROTS, PARSNIPS AND A HONEY AND BALSAMIC GLAZE

2 garlic cloves, peeled and
   crushed
2 fresh thyme sprigs
2 bay leaves
2 wild ducks
4 carrots, peeled and
   thickly sliced
4 parsnips, peeled and
   thickly sliced
2 tbsp runny honey
1 tbsp balsamic vinegar
2 tbsp olive oil
Salt and black pepper to season

serves 4 as a main course

A wild duck has a gamier flavour than a tame duck and much less fat. And that's why they are ideally suited to roasting. They eat particularly well with something sharp and sweet, which in this case, is vinegar and honey.

Preheat oven to 200°C/400°F/Gas Mark 6. Place the garlic, thyme and bay leaves into the cavity of the duck.

Place the duck in a large casserole or roasting tray and seal on all sides with the olive oil over a medium–high heat until golden brown. Remove the ducks from the casserole and pour off half the fat. Add the carrots and allow them to colour slightly, then add the parsnips and toss together. Mix the honey and balsamic vinegar together in a bowl. Once the vegetables have coloured slightly, place the duck on top of the vegetables and brush the honey and balsamic vinegar glaze evenly over. Roast in the hot oven for 18–25 minutes, depending on the size of the duck, basting with the honey and balsamic vinegar glaze frequently.

Remove the duck from oven and leave to rest for 8 minutes, brushing with the glaze.

If the carrots and parsnips are not coloured to your liking, leave them to cook for a couple more minutes while the duck is resting. Season with salt and black pepper.

Carve and serve the duck with the vegetables.

PHEASANT BREAST WITH CAULIFLOWER PURÉE AND ROAST GARLIC

To make your life easier, this sauce can be made a day or two in advance and can easily be frozen. The sauce also goes with most poultry and meat dishes so is a good one to have on standby. In addition, the pheasant can be substituted for partridge or pigeon.

To make the sauce:

Preheat oven to 180°C/350°F/Gas Mark 4. Heat the oil in a large saucepan for 5 minutes. Add the chicken wings and brown over a high heat until coloured. Pour off the excess oil and add the shallots and bay leaves. Cook for 2 minutes.

Deglaze the pan with the Madeira and white wine, then reduce the liquor to half. Add the stock and bring to a near simmer, then simmer for 1 hour, skimming constantly. Strain the sauce into a clean pan, return to the heat, bring back to the boil and skim.

To make the cauliflower purée:

Chop the cauliflower florets into small pieces. Melt a little butter in a medium saucepan, add the shallots and cauliflower and sweat until soft but not coloured. Continue to cook to evaporate the liquid and until the cauliflower is cooked. Transfer the shallots and cauliflower to a blender, add cream as required to blend to a smooth purée (add the cream slowly until the cauliflower starts to purée). Return to a small pan and keep warm.

To roast the garlic:

Place the unpeeled garlic halves cut-side down in a non-stick frying pan. Drizzle over a little olive oil and place over a medium heat until the garlic begins to colour. Place the pan in the hot oven and roast for 8–10 minutes. Remove from oven at the same time as the pheasant and serve.

For the pheasant breast:

Heat a large frying pan. Add the pheasant flesh-side down and cook for 1 minute, or until the skin is golden brown. Turn the pheasant over and transfer the pan to the oven and roast for 5–6 minutes. Remove the pheasant from the oven and leave to rest for 3–4 minutes.

Slice the pheasant and place on 4 individual serving plates. Garnish with thyme sprigs and serve with the sauce, cauliflower purée and roast garlic.

For the sauce

50 ml/2 fl oz olive oil

1 kg/2¼ lb chicken wings

2 shallots, peeled and
  finely sliced

2 bay leaves

75 ml/2½ fl oz Maderia

75 ml/2½ fl oz white wine

1.5 litres/2½ pints chicken stock

For the cauliflower purée

1 head of cauliflower, broken
  into florets

50 g/2 oz butter

2 shallots, peeled and
  finely sliced

4 tbsp double cream

1 head of garlic, cut in half

olive oil, for drizzling

4 pheasant breasts

fresh thyme sprigs, to garnish

serves 4 as a main course

● ● ●   # PIGEON AND FOIE GRAS TART

For the tomato fondue

2 tbsp extra virgin olive oil

1 shallot, peeled and diced

1 garlic clove, peeled and
crushed

1 fresh thyme sprig

1 bay leaf

50 ml/2 fl oz red wine

10 plum tomatoes, peeled and
de-seeded

4 breasts wood pigeon, skin
removed

4 sheets puff pastry

75 g/3 oz baby spinach,
blanched and squeezed to
remove excess moisture

4 x 20 g/¾ oz slices foie gras

1 egg, mixed with fork

2 tbsp milk

50g/1½ oz plain flour

serves 4 as a starter or
main course

What a combination of ingredients this is! The flavours just work so well together. If you don't have time to make the tarts it may be easier to simply pan-fry the pigeon breasts and foie gras and eat them with the spinach.

To make the tomato fondue:

Heat the olive oil in a medium saucepan. Add the shallot and sweat for 2 minutes until soft. Add the garlic, thyme and bay leaf and leave to sweat until soft.

Pour the red wine into the pan and stir to deglaze, then reduce the liquor to a glaze. Add the tomatoes and reduce to a thick paste. Remove the pan from the heat and cool. Transfer to a bowl, cover and leave to chill in the refrigerator until required.

To assemble the tart:

Preheat oven to 220°C/425°F/Gas Mark 7. Heat a non-stick frying pan, add the pigeon breasts and seal on both sides, then remove from the heat and leave to cool. Turn the oven down to 180°C/350°F/Gas Mark 4.

Cut out 8 circles of puff pastry on a lightly floured surface, about 8–10 cm/ 3¼–4 inches in diameter and place 4 pastry discs on greaseproof paper on a baking tray. Place a little spinach in the centre of each pastry disc to form the base of the tart, then place a pigeon breast on top of the spinach. Spread the tomato fondue on the pigeon breast and place the foie gras on top of pigeon. Lay another pastry disc on the top and press down the sides of the pie to make a tart that looks slightly like a ravioli.

Place the tarts in the refrigerator and leave to chill for 30 minutes.

Remove from refrigerator and brush tarts with egg and milk wash and prick the top 3–4 times with a small knife.

Place the tarts on a baking tray and bake in the hot oven for 10–12 minutes until golden brown. Remove from the oven, cut in half and serve immediately.

RABBIT
AND HARE

Whenever I get the chance, I love to cook rabbit and hare. Hares are becoming a protected species in many areas, so please only buy from a reputable supplier. They are very differently flavoured meats. Wild rabbits have a far deeper colour and a much gamier flavour than farmed ones, however I have used farmed rabbits here as these will be easier for you to find.

Different cuts of the animals suit different styles of cooking. The legs are very flavoursome, but are tough so you need to cook them slowly, pot roast, stew or braise. The saddle can be roasted, grilled or poached.

The meat contains very little fat or cholesterol and is high in protein and calcium.

POT ROAST RABBIT WITH BOILED
POTATOES AND POMMERY MUSTARD

When I was a kid I ate a lot of rabbit and the fact that they're now beginning to make a real resurgence makes me happy. The flavour is mild, yet distinct. This is a one-pot wonder with which you can't go wrong.

Preheat oven to 160°C/325°F/Gas Mark 3. Seal the rabbit legs in a large heavy based flameproof casserole until golden brown then remove and set aside.

Melt the butter in the casserole, add the vegetables and leave to sweat for 3–4 minutes. Add the tomatoes and reduce to a paste then add the red wine and stock. Taste and adjust the seasoning if necessary. Return the rabbit legs to the casserole then cook in the hot oven for 30 minutes.

Remove the casserole from the oven, stir in the mustard, then adjust the seasoning and return to oven for further 30 minutes.

Serve the rabbit with boiled potatoes tossed in butter and parsley.

4 hind rabbit legs
4 front rabbit legs
20 g/¾ oz butter
2 shallots, diced
1 small carrot, diced
1 celery rib, diced
1 garlic clove, crushed
white of ½ leek, diced
½ x 250 g/8 oz can tomatoes,
    peeled
100 ml/3½ fl oz red wine
250 ml/8 fl oz chicken stock
2 tbsp pommery or whole-grain
    mustard
1 tbsp fresh flat-leaf parsley,
    finely chopped to serve
boiled potatoes, to serve

serves 4 as a main course

SPINACH TAGLIATELLE WITH RABBIT AND PORCINI MUSHROOMS

In Italy they eat a lot of rabbit with porcini mushrooms and I think the flavours work really well together. If you are not taken by the idea of eating the kidneys and liver, simply leave them out as the dish is just as delicious.

If using the belly flaps, fry in a small frying pan in 2 tbsp olive oil until crisp then slice thinly and return to the pan to make a crispy garnish.

Meanwhile, seal the rabbit loins in a non-stick frying pan for about 2–3 minutes until medium rare. When nearly ready, add the kidneys and livers then remove them from pan and set aside.

Cook the pasta in a large saucepan of boiling salted water until *al dente* (tender but firm to the bite). Drain and set aside.

Return the pan to the heat, add half the olive oil and the shallot and cep (porcini) mushrooms and cook until the mushrooms are caramelized. Add the pasta, herbs and white wine.

Thinly slice the rabbit loin and cut the livers and kidneys in half, then add the meat to the pasta with the butter and toss together.

Transfer to a large serving dish, season with salt and pepper to taste, garnish with shavings of Parmesan and the crispy belly flaps if you like and serve.

2 rabbit belly flaps (optional)
250 g/9 oz fresh spinach
   tagliatelle
salt and freshly ground black
   pepper
1 rabbit saddle, boned into loins
2 rabbit kidneys
2 rabbit livers
100 ml/3½ fl oz extra virgin
   olive oil
1 shallot, peeled and finely diced
400 g/14 oz fresh cep (porcini)
   mushrooms
1 tbsp fresh flat-leaf parsley,
   finely chopped
½ tbsp tarragon leaves
200 ml/7 fl oz white wine
a knob of butter
fresh Parmesan cheese, shavings
   to serve (optional)

serves 4 as a main course

MOSAIC TERRINE OF HARE, FOIE GRAS AND MADEIRA

For the hare stock

1 onion, peeled and diced

2 carrots, peeled and diced

2 celery sticks, diced

2 litres/3½ pints chicken stock

2 fresh thyme sprigs

2 bay leaves

1 hare, legs and fillets removed
   from carcass

20 leaves cavolo nero, julienned

salt

1 x 500–600 g/1 lb 2 oz–1¼ lb
   lobe foie gras

250 ml/8 fl oz Madeira

500 ml/16 fl oz red wine

10 gelatine leaves, soaked
   in cold water

10 slices prosciutto

gherkins, to serve

serves 4 as a starter

This is the most challenging recipe in the book. The good news is, even if a terrine goes a little wrong it should still taste lovely. The art of making terrines is unfortunately being lost, so the satisfaction of getting one that looks great is amazing, believe me. Good luck!

For the hare: Combine all the ingredients for the hare stock in a deep saucepan or stockpot. Bring to the boil and add the hare legs. Reduce to a simmer for about 3½ hours, or until the hare is tender, constantly topping up with water and skimming the surface. Remove hare from the pan and carefully strain the stock. Set aside.

Shred the hare meat from the legs discarding any fat, sinew and bones and leave to chill in the refrigerator.

Blanch the cavolo nero in a medium saucepan of boiling salted water for 1 minute then refresh immediately in ice cold water and place with the hare meat in the refrigerator.

To poach the foie gras and hare fillet: Slice the foie gras into 1 cm/½ inch slices. Bring the hare stock to the boil in a medium saucepan. Add the Madeira and wine to the stock and bring to a simmer. Remove from the heat. Add the foie gras and poach for 2 minutes, then remove from the stock with a slotted spoon, place on a baking tray and leave to cool in the fridge.

Skim the foie gras fat from the top of the stock and return the liquid to a simmer. Add the hare loins and poach for 4–6 minutes until medium rare. Remove the hare loins from the pan and place on the baking tray with the foie gras in the refrigerator.

Measure 1 litre/1¾ pints of stock and season to taste, strain through muslin and return to the boil. Remove from the heat and dissolve the gelatine into the liquid.

To assemble: Line a greased terrine mould with clingfilm. Line the sides of the mould with the prosciutto overlapping the sides of the mould by about 4 cm/1½ inches. It is not necessary to line the ends of the terrine.

Take 75 ml/2½ fl oz of the liquid and pour into the terrine mould and chill until set, about 30 minutes. This creates the base of the terrine.

Layer the inside of the mould alternating with the cavolo nero and shredded hare mixture and the foie gras. Place the hare loins between the layers of foie gras and shredded hare meat. After each layer, pour a small amount, about 150 ml/5 fl oz of the gelatine liquid to cover. After the final layer, pour the remaining liquid into the terrine and fold the overlapping prosciutto over to cover. Leave to set in the refrigerator overnight, or until firm.

Once it has set, turn the terrine out of the mould, place on a chopping board and, using a sharp carving knife, cut into 1 cm/½ inch slices. Serve with some crusty bread and gherkins.

VANILLA

Believe it or not, vanilla is the stamen of a vine orchid plant. Once it is picked the stamen is blanched in boiling water and then left out in the hot sun to dry. Orchids give a low yield of vanilla which is why it is so expensive. To get the vanilla beans out of the pod the best way is to rub it between your forefinger and thumb so as to loosen the beans, then to split the pod with a sharp knife right down the middle. It will then be possible to run the back of a knife down the length of the pod to get the valuable vanilla beans out. The whole pod is then usually placed into the pot.

Vanilla can be used to flavour a number of things such as sugar. All you do is put a couple of the vanilla pods into a jar of sugar and cover with an airtight lid. The vanilla is so strong in aroma that the flavour will permeate easily and quickly.

● ○ ○ ## VANILLA STOCK SYRUP

1 litre/1¾ pints water
1 kg/2 lb caster sugar
1 lemon, cut in half lengthways
   and sliced
4 vanilla pods

makes 1 litre/1¾ pints

A stock syrup is a staple of every good pastry kitchen. It can be served warm over ice cream and fresh fruits or used to poach all sorts of fruits like pears and peaches. Because of its high level of sugar it will keep in the refrigerator for up to 3–4 weeks.

Bring all the ingredients to the boil in a large saucepan for 5 minutes.

Remove from the heat and pour the syrup into sterilized bottles. Push the lemon slices and vanilla pods into the bottles.

It can be stored in the refrigerator for up to a month. Stock syrup can be served with anything sweet from ice cream to fresh fruit, or it can be used to poach fruits like peaches or pears.

VANILLA PANNACOTTA
WITH PEAR POACHED IN CIDER

● ● ○

You can poach fruit in almost anything that tastes good. In the UK I am really lucky to have good tasting cider on my doorstep. I have decided to pay homage to this and the results are great!

To make the poaching liquid:

Bring all the ingredients to the boil in a large saucepan. Add the pears and cook at a gentle simmer for 10–20 minutes (cooking time will be determined by the ripeness of the pears).

Leave the pears to cool in the poaching liquid and place in the refrigerator overnight.

Take 150 ml/5 fl oz of the poaching liquid, reduce by two thirds until liquid resembles a glaze and set aside to drizzle over the finished dish.

To make the pannacotta:

Warm the cream, sugar and vanilla pod in a medium saucepan and bring to a near simmer.

Once the sugar has dissolved, slowly add the softened gelatine, stirring constantly until the gelatine has dissolved. Strain the cream through a fine sieve, then pour the cream into 4–6 dariole moulds and leave to set in the refrigerator for 2–3 hours.

Once the pannacotta has set, remove them from the moulds by dipping the moulds into a large pan of hot water and turning the panna cotta out onto individual serving plates.

Remove the pears from the poaching liquid and use a small knife to fan the base of the pear. Place a pear on the serving plate with the pannacotta and serve with a drizzle of the reduced poaching liquid.

For the poaching liquid
150 g/5 oz light muscovado (brown) sugar
500 ml/16 fl oz cider
2 oranges, zest and juice of
1 vanilla pod, split lengthways
4 pears, peeled and cores removed with melon baller

For the vanilla pannacotta
250 ml/8 fl oz double cream
30 g/1 oz caster sugar
1 vanilla pod, split lengthways
1 gelatine leaf, soaked in cold water to soften

serves 4

● ● ●

CLASSIC APPLE TARTE TATIN
WITH VANILLA ICE CREAM

200 g/7 oz butter

200 g/7 oz caster sugar

4 apples, peeled, cored and cut
into halves

1 cinnamon stick, broken in half

2 vanilla pods, split lengthways

2 x 18 cm/7 inch puff pastry
discs, rolled to a thickness
of 3 mm/⅛ inch

For the caramel sauce

200 g/7 oz caster sugar

100 ml/3 ½ fl oz double cream

vanilla ice cream, to serve

Makes 2 tartes, to serve 4

A tarte tatin was invented by mistake. It's a tart that is almost cooked upside down so the caramel forms in the base of the pan cooking the apples while the pastry sits above the apples trapping in the beautiful flavours. What a fantastic mistake to make!

Using 2 x 15 cm/6 inch high-sided copper pans or high-sided saucepans, spread 100 g/3½ oz of the butter over the base of each pan. Sprinkle 100 g/3½ oz sugar over the butter in each pan, then place 4 apple halves, core-side facing up, on top of the butter and sugar in each pan. Place a cinnamon stick piece and vanilla pod in between the apple halves in the shape of a cross.

Stretch the pastry over the apples pushing the pastry down between the apples and the sides of the pans. Prick the pastry 4–5 times with a fork, then leave the tarte tatins to rest for 1 hour in the refrigerator.

Preheat oven to 180°C/350°F/Gas Mark 4. To cook the tarte tatins, begin to caramelize the sugar and butter over a medium–high heat, on preferably an electric hob or barbecue. You won't be able to see the full extent of the sugar colouring but if you gently swirl the pan, you will get glimpses down the side of the pastry – it should take 4–5 minutes. Transfer to the hot oven and cook until the pastry is golden brown, about 18–22 minutes. Remove from the oven and leave to stand for about 1 hour to allow the flavours to amalgamate.

To make the caramel sauce:

Heat the sugar in a saucepan over a medium–high heat until it has dissolved. Once the sugar has melted and begins to change colour, you will need to keep a careful eye on it as it will change colour and burn quickly. As soon as the sugar turns golden brown, add the cream. Remove the saucepan from the heat and leave to cool slightly.

To serve: Place the tarte tatins over a high heat and heat until the caramel in the base begins to bubble. In one swift movement, turn the tarte tatins over onto a serving plate, discarding the vanilla and cinnamon stick. If the plate is messy, it may be easier to transfer to a clean plate to serve. Drizzle the caramel sauce around the tarte tatins and serve with a scoop of vanilla ice cream.

WINTER

When winter hits it can hit fairly hard. You get to sport big coats, scarves and gloves and hurry from one place to the other as quickly as possible because it's so cold. This type of weather is perfect for hearty soups, braised meats and risottos. The food needs to warm you up and make you content.

I think after a cold day we need to light the fire or crank up the heating, have a warm bath and then think about dinner.

Dinner may take a bit longer to prepare during winter but that doesn't mean that you have to be in the kitchen all evening. The great thing about winter food is a lot of it can even be prepared the previous day, like soups, stews and pot roasts.

Truffles come into season during winter, so if you are looking to splash out on a big dinner or enjoy a little decadence as opposed to going out to an expensive restaurant then this is the time of year to do it. There is a lot to choose from for the meat lovers with beef and oxtail at its best and game is still around. Vegetarians certainly don't miss out either, with some of the most beautiful mushrooms around and gutsy lentil soups which are a meal on their own.

Last, and most certainly not least, it's time to eat chocolate. I don't care if it's my flourless chocolate and pecan torte or a simple hot chocolate, you deserve it – enjoy!

TRUFFLES

Truffles are a type of fungus that grow attached to tree roots. When the truffles are ripe they have a strong aroma hence historically, pigs were used to snuffle them out. These days dogs are trained to find them. This time-consuming method of finding truffles makes these rare little gems so expensive. There are more than fifty different varieties of truffles with long and complicated names, so I will keep it simple for you. The two varieties that you need to look for are both from Europe – the white truffle from Alba (Italy) and the black winter truffle. The white truffle from Alba is the daddy of all truffles. They are easily the most expensive, (in 2005) selling for up to £1,200 per kilo. The price fluctuates with the supply and demand. The truffles should be shaved raw over something very simple like a plain risotto or some pasta. The winter truffle, which grows in parts of Italy and France can either be cooked in a Madeira and veal stock or may be shaved raw as the white. However you eat them you'll be amazed at how good they are.

● ○ ○ ## SCRAMBLED EGGS WITH BLACK TRUFFLES

12 eggs
600 ml/1 pint double cream
1 black truffle
1 tbsp fresh flat-leaf parsley,
   coarsely chopped
10 g/¼ oz butter
bread, to serve

serves 4–6 as a starter

I serve this in the restaurant as a starter and it always goes down a treat, but, if you're looking for serious brownie points, try serving it for breakfast with a glass of champagne. If you can't afford the truffles, you can always substitute them with smoked salmon.

Crack the eggs into a bowl, add the cream and mix until combined. Chop half of the black truffle and finely slice the rest. Combine the chopped truffle in a separate bowl with the parsley and set the sliced truffle aside for the garnish.

Melt butter in a large non stick pan over a medium heat and add the egg mixture. Don't stir the eggs for 30 seconds, then start to gently move the egg mixture around the pan with a wooden spoon, creating curds of egg.

Toast the bread and place the eggs on the toast. Garnish with the remaining sliced truffle and serve.

TAGLIATELLE OF WHITE TRUFFLES FROM ALBA

● ● ○

If you ever get the chance to cook with these white truffles, try them this way first. The flavour of the white truffles is so good it's almost indescribable and there's nothing better than home-made tagliatelle to show off that flavour. If you're really pushed for time, you can buy fresh pasta from a good quality Italian deli.

For the pasta dough:

Combine the flour, egg yolks, egg and olive oil in a large mixing bowl. Mix with your hands to combine all the ingredients. Knead the mixture until the dough resembles a smooth paste-like texture then cover the dough with clingfilm and leave to rest in refrigerator for 1 hour.

Using a pasta machine, roll the dough until it is 1–2 mm/⅟₁₆ inch thick. Use the attachment on the machine to then cut the dough into 1 mm/⅟₃₂ inch wide strips.

Cook the tagliatelle in a large saucepan of boiling salted water until until *al dente* (tender but firm to the bite). If you are using home-made pasta, this will only take 20–30 seconds.

Melt the butter in a separate medium-large saucepan and slowly add the hot water, stirring constantly to make an emulsion.

Drain the pasta and add it to the emulsion. Season with salt and pepper, add the chopped parsley and toss until the pasta is coated.

Twist the tagliatelle around a roasting fork and place it onto individual serving plates. Finely slice the truffle over the pasta and serve.

For the pasta dough
550 g/1⅔ lb Italian "00" flour
6 egg yolks
4 whole eggs
2 tbsp extra virgin olive oil

320 g/11½ oz dried tagliatelle
salt and freshly ground black
    pepper
40 g/1½ oz butter
2 tbsp hot water
1 tbsp fresh flat-leaf parsley,
    coarsely chopped
100 g/3½ oz white truffles,
    finely sliced

serves 4–6 as a starter
    or main course

POT AU FEU OF LOBSTER, LANGOUSTINE AND SCALLOP WITH FOIE GRAS AND BLACK TRUFFLES

For the stock

2.5 kg/5½ lb veal bones

5 litres/8¾ pints water

2 leeks, coarsely chopped

1 celery stick, chopped

2 onions, peeled and chopped

2 bay leaves

2 fresh thyme sprigs

½ bunch of fresh parsley stalks

1 fresh lobster

1 each of carrot, shallot and celery
stick, peeled and chopped

4 scallops

4 x 30 g/1 oz foie gras

8 langoustines

12 each of baby turnips, baby
leeks and baby carrots, peeled
and shaped

1 black truffle, very finely sliced

fresh chervil and tarragon leaves,
to garnish

serves 4 as a main course

This dish is certainly one to pull out if you're trying to impress. It uses the best and most luxurious ingredients in a fairly simple way so the quality and taste of the ingredients can shine through. You will need to save your pennies but by God its worth it!

To make the stock:

Rinse the veal bones under running water. Place the bones in a large stockpot and fill with cold water. There should be twice as much water as there is bones. Bring to the boil and as soon as the pot begins to simmer, remove from the heat. Drain and rinse the bones well, ensuring all impurities are removed and discard liquid. Clean the pot, return the bones to it and cover with water. While slowly bringing the water to a simmer and constantly skimming, add the vegetables and herbs and simmer gently for 4–5 hours. Strain the stock carefully through muslin.

To blanch the lobster:

Bring a large saucepan of water to the boil with the carrot, shallot and celery. Remove from the heat, leave to cool for 60 seconds, then place the lobster in the pan for 3 minutes. If you buy the lobster alive a humane way to kill

it is to place it in the freezer to fall asleep.

Once the lobster has been in the water for 3 minutes, remove it and leave to cool on a baking tray in the refrigerator for 10 minutes.

Take the lobster's claws out of the shell, and cut the lobster tail into 4 medallions, cutting through the shell at the joints. Set the claw meat and lobster medallions aside.

Place 2–3 litres/3½–5 pints of the veal stock in a medium to large pan and bring to a near simmer. Place the lobster and scallops in the pan for 2 minutes, then add the foie gras and poach for 2 minutes. Add the langoustines and poach for a further 3 minutes.

Remove all the ingredients from the pan and replace with the baby leeks and carrots, bringing the pan of stock to the boil. Arrange the shellfish and lobster in and around 4 deep bowls, garnish with the vegetables and spoon the stock over. Thinly shave truffles over the dish, garnish with the herb leaves and serve.

LENTILS

Lentils come in five or six different colours ranging from red to yellow to green. I like to cook with the green varieties, Casteluccio or Puy lentils. The Puy lentils are a little darker in colour and have been dried out a little more. The Casteluccio lentils come from a small village in Umbria, which is truffle country in Italy.

Lentils take 35–40 minutes to cook and the green variety keep their shape once cooked. I used to think of lentils as veggie food with very little taste. It wasn't until a holiday in the south of France that I discovered how amazing they can be when cooked in flavour-filled stocks.

A good source of cholesterol-lowering fibre, high in the B vitamins, protein, magnesium and iron, almost fat free and containing favourable amounts of folic acid.

● ○ ○

LENTIL STEW WITH SPICY SAUSAGE

2 shallots, peeled and sliced
2 small carrots, peeled and
    finely diced
3 bay leaves
2 x 400 g/14 oz cans tomatoes
200 ml/7 fl oz red wine
400 g/14 oz Castelluccio lentils
700 ml/1¼ pints chicken stock
150 g/5 oz spicy sausage
salt and freshly ground black
    pepper

serves 4–6 as a main course

I'm lucky enough to have this spicy sausage brought to me from Calabria in the south of Italy where I first tasted it with my great mate Tomaso. If you can't get your hands on it, it's possible to use a chorizo. This can be served on its own or as an accompaniment to something like roast duck.

Preheat oven to 180°C/350°F/Gas Mark 4. Heat 2 tbsp of oil in a large casserole and sweat the shallots and carrot with the bay leaf until soft. Add the tomatoes and reduce until the mixture begins to stick to base of the casserole.

Pour in the wine and stir to deglaze, then reduce the liquor by half. Add the lentils and stock and cook in the hot oven for 20 minutes. Fry the sausage in a frying pan, then add to the lentil stew. Return to oven for a further 15 minutes. Check the seasoning and serve.

ZUPPA RIBOLATA
(LENTIL SOUP WITH VEGETABLES)

I am a self-confessed meat-lover. Even though this soup is ideal to serve to vegans, it is so flavoursome that I would not hesitate to serve it at a cattle farmer's meeting!

For the purée:

Place the lentils and the 325 ml/11 fl oz stock in a large saucepan and cook over a low heat until all the liquid has evaporated and the lentils are tender, about 25 minutes.

Remove from the heat, transfer the lentils to a blender and process, adding enough extra stock as needed, until smooth. Set the purée aside until required.

For the soup:

Heat the olive oil in a pan, add the carrots, celery, shallots, leek and garlic and sweat for 5 minutes over a low heat. Add the lentils, bay leaf and thyme and the measured water and bring to the boil. Simmer for about 25 minutes, or until lentils are soft. Skim any impurities from the surface of the soup, and add the cavolo nero. Cook for a further 5 minutes, or until the cabbage is cooked.

Check the seasoning, add the reserved purée, garnish with croûtons and serve.

For the purée

125 g/4 oz Castelluccio lentils
325 ml/11 fl oz vegetable stock
150 ml/5 fl oz vegetable stock,
   to purée the lentils

For the soup

2 tbsp olive oil
2 small carrots, peeled and diced
1½ celery sticks, diced
3 shallots, peeled and diced
1 leek, white only, diced
3 garlic cloves, peeled and
   chopped
200 g/7 oz lentils
1.2 litres/2 pints water
1 bay leaf
1 fresh thyme sprig
8 leaves cavolo nero, thinly sliced
salt and freshly ground black
   pepper
croûtons, to garnish

serves 4–6 as a starter
   or main course

PAN-FRIED CALVES' LIVER WITH PANCETTA, SAGE AND LENTILS

For the sauce
125 ml/4 fl oz white wine
125 ml/4 fl oz white wine vinegar
3 shallots, peeled and finely sliced
500 g/1 lb 2 oz chicken wings
2 tbsp olive oil
1 garlic clove, crushed
100 g/3½ oz button mushrooms,
  sliced
1 fresh thyme sprig
700 ml/1¼ pints chicken stock
50 g/2 oz butter

12 thin slices pancetta
12 fresh sage leaves
olive oil
½ shallot, peeled and finely diced
½ carrot, peeled and finely diced
1 garlic clove, crushed
250 g/9 oz Puy lentils
200 ml/7 fl oz white wine
200 ml/7 fl oz double cream
4 x 140–160 g/4½–5½ oz slices
  calves' liver
salt and freshly ground black pepper
100 g/3½ oz plain flour

serves 4 as a main course

I believe liver is a bit like vegemite or marmite, you either love it or hate it. The silly thing is though, many people already have an opinion on liver before they have even tasted it. Liver is full of iron and served with a sauce like this one, it is absolutely delicious!

Preheat oven to 180°C/350°F/Gas Mark 4.

For the sauce:
Place the white wine, white wine vinegar and 1 of the sliced shallots in a large saucepan, then bring to the boil for 10 minutes and reduce by half. Strain and set this reduction aside until required.

Brown the chicken wings in pre-heated oil in a large saucepan, then pour off the excess oil. Add the remaining shallots and garlic and cook until coloured. Add the mushrooms, herbs, peppercorns and strained reduction and reduce by one-quarter. Add the stock and simmer for 30 minutes.

Pass the sauce through a sieve and before serving, whisk in the butter.

Place the pancetta on a flat baking tray and place in the hot oven until crispy. Take a dinner plate and wrap clingfilm over the surface to give a completely smooth top. Dip the sage leaves in a little olive oil (2 tsp) and place them "pretty-side" down on the plate. Place the plate in the microwave on high power for about 1 minute, or until sage leaves are crisp. Set aside.

Sweat the shallots, carrots and garlic with 1 tbsp olive oil in a medium pan. Add the lentils, then pour in the white wine and stir to deglaze. Reduce the liquor, then add one cup of water and cook for 8–10 minutes. Add the double cream and cook slowly for 15–20 minutes. Season the calves' liver with salt and pepper, dust with flour and shake off the excess.

Heat a non-stick frying pan, add the liver and cook for 1–2 minutes on each side.

Place the lentils on individual serving plates and arrange the liver on top. Drizzle the sauce, having added the butter, around the plates and serve. Use the crispy sage leaves as a garnish.

MUSHROOMS

Mushrooms come in so many shapes, sizes, colours and flavours – there are 1,900 varieties that we currently know about. They range in taste from very delicate to blow your head off with flavour. There is a mushroom for everybody and everything. So if you see a type of mushroom that you have not yet tasted – give it a go!

The easiest way to split mushrooms is into cultivated and wild. The wild mushrooms are different species that we can grow under controlled conditions. It's for this reason that they are much more expensive but very flavoursome. Cultivated mushrooms are also great, with each variety having its own distinctive taste.

High in selenium and potassium and very high in iron, zinc and the B vitamins.

● ○ ○ CREAMY SOUP OF FIELD MUSHROOMS

2 shallots, finely sliced
1 leek, white portion only,
  finely sliced
40 g/1½ oz butter
550 g/1⅔ lb field mushrooms,
  finely sliced
1 litre/1¾ pints chicken stock
100 g/3½ oz potato, finely sliced
500 ml/16 fl oz double cream
400 ml/14 fl oz milk
To garnish
cep (porcini) mushrooms
fresh chervil sprigs

serves 4 as a starter

I serve this soup in every restaurant that I cook at because it's so easy to make. It rarely gets served without a compliment. So, if you like soup, then please try this one.

Melt the butter in a large saucepan, add the shallots and leek and sweat for 2 minutes. Add the field mushrooms and cook for a further 10 minutes until most of the moisture has evaporated.

Place the chicken stock and potato slices in a separate saucepan and leave to simmer until the potato is soft. Pour the stock and potato into the mushrooms and bring to a rapid boil. Add the cream and milk and bring the soup to a gentle simmer for 10 minutes. Don't allow it to boil.

Transfer the mixture to a blender and process until smooth, then return to a clean saucepan and reheat gently. Using a hand-held blender, pulse to create a frothy foam.

Pour the soup into 4 serving bowls, garnish with cep (porcini) mushrooms and chervil, and serve immediately.

SAUTÉED WILD MUSHROOMS ON FRIED CIABATTA WITH A POACHED HENS EGG

I get so excited about wild mushrooms. When one mushroom season finishes, another begins. It doesn't matter what kind of mushrooms you can get your hands on for this recipe, any of them will fit the bill!

Place a large high-sided saucepan over a medium–high heat and fill (nearly) to the top with water. Add the white wine vinegar and bring to the boil.

Place a large frying pan over a medium–high heat and melt the butter. Add the shallot and garlic and leave to sweat for 1-2 minutes. Add the mushrooms, toss in the pan with the parsley until the herb is evenly distributed and season with salt and pepper.

Meanwhile, break the eggs into the boiling water and poach for 2 minutes.

Toss the mushrooms and add the parsley. Place the ciabatta slices on a griddle pan, drizzle with a little olive oil and grill until toasted.

Place the toasted ciabatta on serving plates and top with the sautéed mushrooms and poached eggs. Drizzle with olive oil and serve.

175 ml/6 fl oz white wine vinegar
75 g/3 oz butter
½ shallot, peeled and finely chopped
½ garlic clove, peeled and finely chopped
400 g/14 oz assorted wild mushrooms
salt and freshly ground black pepper
4 free-range eggs
1 tbsp fresh flat-leaf parsley, finely sliced
4 slices of ciabatta
extra virgin olive oil, for drizzling

serves 4 as a starter

RISOTTO OF CONFIT DUCK
AND WILD MUSHROOMS

For the confit duck

2 duck legs

80 g/3¼ oz rock salt

1 fresh thyme sprig

2 bay leaves

10 peppercorns

zest of ½ orange

500 g/1 lb 2 oz duck fat

For the mushroom stock

2 tbsp olive oil

1 onion, peeled and diced

mushroom trimmings (see below)

1 bay leaf

2 fresh thyme sprigs

1.5 litres/2½ pints water

2 tbsp extra virgin olive oil

2 small shallots, finely sliced

3 garlic cloves, crushed

400 g/14 oz vialone nano or
    other risotto rice

1 fresh thyme sprig

2 bay leaves

200 ml/7 fl oz red wine

100 g/3½ oz butter

150 g/5 oz mixed wild mushrooms,
    cleaned, trimmed and sliced

75 g/3 oz freshly grated
    Parmesan cheese

20 g/¾ oz mascarpone

shavings of Parmesan cheese

salt and pepper to taste

serves 4 as a main course

The only reason that I classify this recipe as adventurous is because the confit duck takes 2½ hours to make. If you are pushed for time, you can try and buy the confit duck and substitute the mushroom stock for a store-bought chicken stock.

To confit the duck legs:

Place the duck legs in a large bowl with all the confit ingredients, except the duck fat. Massage the duck with the ingredients and leave to rest for 8–12 hours in the refrigerator.

Preheat oven to 150°C/300°F/Gas Mark 2. Remove the duck from the refrigerator and rinse under cold running water.

Place the duck legs in a large roasting tin and cover with the duck fat. Place in the oven and cook for 2½ hours, or until the meat falls away from the bone.

Remove the duck from the fat and leave until cool enough to handle. Turn the oven up to 180°C/350°F/Gas Mark 4. Place the duck legs skin-side down in a non-stick frying pan and return to the oven for 5–6 minutes until the skin is cripsy. The duck fat can be re-used for roasting potatoes.

For the mushroom stock:

Heat the olive oil in a large saucepan. Add the onion and sweat until soft. Add all the mushroom trimmings, excluding any dark mushrooms such as trompette de la mortes and lightly cook until the liquid has evaporated. Add the bay leaf, thyme sprigs and the water, then bring to the boil and leave to simmer for 20 minutes. Strain and set aside.

To make the risotto:

Heat the olive oil in a medium-large saucepan. Add the shallots and garlic and sweat until soft. Add the rice, thyme sprig and bay leaf and stir for 30 seconds. Pour in the red wine and stir to deglaze, then slowly start adding the reserved stock a ladleful at a time, stirring constantly.

Melt 20 g/¾ oz of the butter in a separate pan. Add the mushrooms and sauté for 2-3 minutes until soft. Set aside.

When the rice is almost ready, add the mushrooms, setting a few aside for the garnish. Check the rice and once it is *al dente* (tender but firm to the bite), remove from the heat and add the Parmesan, mascarpone and remaining butter. Season to taste. Stir until combined. Place the duck legs on top of the risotto, garnish with the reserved wild mushrooms and serve with Parmesan shavings.

COD

Cod has a long history in Europe for all sorts of reasons. Many decades ago, British fishing vessels and the Icelandic coastguard went head to head over who was allowed to fish in which areas. This even caused some ships to be capsized and the dispute to be dubbed the Cod Wars. So what were they fighting for? A lovely white-fleshed fish that thrives in colder waters. Cod is one of the most versatile fish money can buy. It's great deep-fried, roasted, poached, steamed or even turned into a soup.

High in protein, selenium and niacin, omega-3 fatty acids and vitamins D, B12 and B6.

BEER-BATTERED COD WITH HOME-MADE CHIPS AND TARTARE SAUCE

● ○ ○

Some things should never be changed. My Dad used to allow my brother Luke and I to have fish and chips every Friday night. What can I say, old habits die hard. I love fish and chips and now you can see just how easy it is to make them at home!

Place mayonnaise in a bowl, stir in the parsley, gherkins and capers, then season the fish with salt and pepper to taste and set aside.

Combine the lager and yeast in another bowl and leave in a warm place for 15–20 minutes.

Cut the potatoes into chips and blanch in a saucepan of boiling water for 4 minutes. Drain and leave to cool.

Using a whisk, slowly mix the lager and yeast together, then gradually add the flour. Cover with a wet dish towel and leave to rise for 10–15 minutes.

Heat the oil for deep-frying in a deep-fat fryer or deep saucepan to 170°C/340°F or until a cube of bread browns in 30 seconds. Dip the fish into the batter, dust with flour and shake off any excess. Carefully lower the fish into the oil and deep fry for 3 minutes or until golden brown. Remove with a slotted spoon and drain on kitchen paper.

Deep-fry the potato chips in vegetable oil until golden and crispy and drain on kitchen paper.

Place the fish and chips on individual serving plates, garnish with a few parsley leaves and lemon wedges and serve with the tartare sauce.

250 ml/8 fl oz mayonnaise (see recipe on page 91)
1 tbsp fresh flat-leaf parsley, chopped
100 g/3½ oz gherkins, chopped
20 extra fine capers, chopped
salt and freshly ground black pepper
440 ml/15 fl oz lager
1 tsp dried yeast
4 large jacket potatoes
300 g/11 oz plain flour
4 x 170 g/6 oz cod portions
oil, for deep-frying
fresh flat-leaf parsley leaves
lemon wedges

serves 4 as a main course

CURRY-INFUSED COD WITH
BRAISED LEEKS AND CRISPY POTATOES

● ● ○

In this recipe, the curry-flavoured oil is used to infuse the cod so as not to overpower the lovely taste of the fish. For anyone who finds normal curries a little hot, this dish is a great way to introduce yourself to the flavour.

Place all the spices in a small saucepan and place over a low–medium heat for 2 minutes until the spices are lightly toasted. Remove from the heat and add the groundnut (peanut) oil. Leave to infuse for 24 hours.

Strain the oil and pour over the cod in a shallow dish, then leave to marinate in the refrigerator for 12 hours.

Heat 2 tbsp olive oil in a pan, add the carrot, celery, garlic and onion and sweat for 3 minutes, then add the leeks and chicken stock.

Once the liquid comes to a simmer, reduce the heat and simmer slowly for 8 minutes, or until all vegetables are tender.

Cook the potatoes in a saucepan of boiling water for 12–15 minutes, or until just cooked. Remove and leave to cool. Once cool, place the potatoes on a chopping (cutting) board and squash flat (you may like to use a saucepan to do this).

Heat a frying pan then add a little olive oil and fry the potatoes until crispy.

Heat another non-stick pan and fry the fish for 2–3 minutes on each side until cooked and a cocktail stick (toothpick) inserted into the thickest part of the fillet offers no resistance.

Remove the veggies from pan and add butter to liquid, stirring with a whisk.

Serve the cod, potatoes and leeks together with a little of the braising liquid from the leeks.

1 tsp turmeric
1 tsp ground cumin
1 tsp paprika
1 tsp fennel seeds, ground
1 coriander seeds, ground
2 tsp curry powder
100 ml/3½ fl oz groundnut oil
4 x 175 g/6 oz cod portions, skin on
olive oil
1 carrot, peeled and cut into thin strips
1 celery stick, cut into thin strips
2 garlic cloves, peeled and finely chopped
1 onion, peeled and finely chopped
12 baby leeks, trimmed
1 leek, cut into thin strips
300 ml/10 fl oz chicken stock
20 baby potatoes
2 tbsp butter

serves 4 as a main course

● ● ●   # SOUP OF SALTED COD WITH BRANDADE AND CROÛTONS

100 g/3½ oz rock salt
1 x 1 kg/2¼ lb cod fillet
25 g/1 oz butter
1 shallot, peeled and sliced
200 g/7 oz leek, white only
1 fresh thyme sprig
½ garlic clove, peeled and
  crushed
zest of 1 orange, finely grated
1.5 litres/2½ pints fish stock
  or water
100 g/3½ oz potato, peeled and
  finely sliced
450 ml/15 fl oz double cream
1 thin French bread stick
1 garlic clove, peeled and
  cut in half
oilve oil, for drizzling

serves 4 as a starter

The only reason I classify this recipe as adventurous is because of the time it takes to make the salt cod. A much quicker alternative is to buy salt cod from a good Italian delicatessen and then wash the salt off as detailed below.

Place the cod in a shallow dish and sprinkle it with salt until completely covered. Cover in clingfilm and leave in refrigerator for 6 hours. A lot of moisture will come out of the cod.

Wash the salt off the cod by leaving it under running water for about 30 minutes. (Alternatively, place the cod in a bowl of cold water for 30 minutes before changing the water. Repeat this 4 times.) Pat the cod dry, remove and discard the skin from the cod and dice into 1 cm/½ inch pieces.

Melt a little butter in a large heavy based pan, add the shallot, leek, thyme and garlic and leave to sweat in butter until soft but not coloured.

Add the salt cod and grated orange zest and sweat for a further 5 minutes. Add the stock or water and the potato slices and bring to the boil. Then leave to simmer for 5 minutes, then add the cream and return to a soft simmer. Remove the pan from the heat and leave to cool.

Transfer the soup to a blender and process until smooth, then pass through a fine sieve into a clean saucepan. Set aside the purée (this is the brandade). Reheat the soup gently and, using a hand-held blender, pulse to a frothy foam.

Preheat the grill. Cut the thin bread stick into thin croûtons. Rub each croûton with half a cut garlic clove and drizzle with a little olive oil. Cook under the grill until golden brown.

Place a small spoonful of brandade on each croûton then sit them on top of the soup. Serve.

BEEF AND OXTAIL

British beef is up there with the best in the world. The lovely green pastures that the cattle graze on are one reason for its outstanding quality. The ageing of beef done by butchers is also very important. Beef needs to be hung and aged for a period of time to promote tenderness and flavour. The longer the beef is hung the more expensive it becomes as it loses weight and is costly to keep in stock. I believe that beef should be hung for between 25–30 days. The more work a particular muscle does the greater its flavour, although the tougher it will become. Therefore cuts from the forequarter, tail and legs are better suited to slower cooking methods like braising, stewing etc. I love cooking beef, whether it's roasting on the bone, or sealing a fillet to be served as a carpaccio.

A good source of protein, iron, vitamins B2, B3, B6, B12, phosphorus, zinc and selenium.

● ○ ○ ## PEPPERED SIRLOIN STEAK
WITH CARAMELIZED SPROUTS

400 g/14 oz Brussel sprouts
salt and black pepper
10 g/¼ oz black peppercorns, crushed
4 x 220 g/7½ oz sirloin steaks
100 g/3½ oz butter
100 ml/3½ fl oz red wine
extra virgin olive oil

serves 4 as a main course

I've always been lucky enough to love Brussel sprouts, but not everyone does. That is, until they've eaten them this way. This dish is the healthy version of steak and chips and I think it tastes even better.

Blanch the Brussel sprouts in a large saucepan of boiling salted water for 2–3 minutes, then refresh in ice cold water. Cut the sprouts in half and remove any outer leaves.

Sprinkle the crushed peppercorns over a large plate. Press each steak into the crushed pepper, then season both sides with salt.

Heat a large frying pan, add the olive oil and when hot, add the steaks and cook for 2 minutes on each side.

Place half the butter and Brussel sprouts in a separate preheated frying pan and allow to caramelize for 2 minutes. Season with salt and pepper to taste.

Add the red wine and remaining butter to the steaks and remove the pan from the heat. Divide the Brussel sprouts between 4 serving plates, then place the steaks on top. Spoon the pan juices over the beef and serve immediately.

SLOWLY BRAISED OXTAIL
WITH POMME DAUPHINOISE

● ● ○

Because the tail is such an active part of the ox, the meat is extremely tough but also very flavoursome. This slow method of cooking means that you end up with a beautifully flavoured meat that falls off the bone.

In a casserole dish marinate the oxtail in the red wine, garlic and thyme overnight.

The next day, remove the oxtail from the marinade, strain and reserve. Pat dry the oxtail of any excess marinade with kitchen paper.

Season the oxtail with salt and pepper and dust the oxtail in flour. Shake to remove any excess.

Heat a large flameproof casserole and brown the oxtail on all sides with olive oil, then remove from the casserole and discard half of the oil.

Add the carrots, shallots, thyme sprigs and bay leaves and celery and cook until coloured then remove and set aside. Wipe out any excess oil or fat from the casserole and return the oxtail to the casserole. Pour in the reserved marinade and stir to deglaze, then bring the liquor to the boil. Skim away any impurities with a slotted spoon, then reduce the heat so that the liquid is not quite simmering. Continue topping up with water and skimming off the fat

as required for 2½ hours. The oxtail should be kept covered by water throughout cooking.

Add the reserved vegetables and leave to simmer for a further 20 minutes. Strain off the liquid into a saucepan and reduce this to a sauce-like consistency over a high heat. Keep the oxtail hot by covering and keeping in a warm place.

For the Dauphinoise:

Preheat oven to 180ºC/350°F/Gas Mark 4. Layer the potatoes in a large flameproof casserole. Combine the cream and milk and season with salt and pepper to taste and pour over the potatoes.

Cover the casserole with the lid and cook in the oven for 1 hour. Remove the lid and cook for a further 30 minutes until golden brown.

To serve: Place 2–3 pieces of the oxtail in each serving bowl with some of the vegetables. Pour the strained sauce over the oxtail and vegetables and serve with potatoes Dauphinoise.

1.5 kg/3¼ lb oxtail, cut into
  5–6 cm/2–2½ inch lengths
375 ml/13 fl oz red wine
3 garlic cloves, peeled and crushed
2 fresh thyme sprigs
salt and freshly ground black pepper
100 g/3½ oz plain flour
75 ml/2½ fl oz olive oil
2 medium carrots, peeled and cut
  into large dice
3 shallots, peeled and cut into
  large dice
2 ribs celery, cut into large dice
3 bay leaves
4 fresh thyme sprigs

For the Dauphinoise
6 x 300 g/11 oz baking potatoes,
  sliced into thick matchsticks
300 ml/10 fl oz double cream
100 ml/3½ fl oz milk

serves 4 as a main course

● ● ●

STANDING ROAST RIB OF BEEF
WITH DIJON, GARLIC AND YORKSHIRE PUDDINGS

As soon as I moved to the UK, I fell in love with the way they have Sunday roasts. It's an absolute must on Sundays and nothing beats a standing rib roasted on the bone.

For the Yorkshire puddings

7 eggs
375 g/13 oz plain flour
750 ml/1¼ pints milk
vegetable oil, for cooking

For the creamed horseradish

250 ml/8 fl oz whipping cream
½ medium–large horseradish, peeled and finely grated
salt and freshly ground black pepper

1 x 1.8 kg–2 kg/4–4½ lb standing rib of beef
3 carrots, peeled and coarsely cut
3 celery ribs, coarsely cut
4 shallots, peeled and cut into quarters lengthways
½ bunch of fresh thyme
75 g/3 oz Dijon mustard
watercress, to garnish

serves 4 as a main course

To make the Yorkshire puddings:

Preheat oven to 200°C/400°F/Gas Mark 6. Using a whisk, combine the eggs and flour in a large mixing bowl. Still whisking, add the milk gradually until smooth and not lumpy. The more the batter is worked in the early stage of making it, the better the puddings will rise when cooked in the oven. Season with a little salt and set aside to rest for 1 hour.

Pour a little vegetable oil into 4 small bellini pans or muffin tins, about 8 cm/3¼ inches in diameter, then pour about 50 ml/2 fl oz of the batter into the pans. Place the pans on a baking tray and cook in the oven for 10–12 minutes.

When the pudding has formed its sides and turned a light golden brown, remove the rack, lift the puddings out of the bellini pans or muffin tins and return them to the rack upside down for 1–2 minutes to dry them out. Once the puddings have been taken from the oven they can be cooled and reheated before serving.

To make the horseradish cream:

Semi-whip the cream in a bowl. Stir in the horseradish and season with salt and pepper.

To roast the beef:

Reduce the oven temperature to 180°C/350°F/Gas Mark 4. Season the beef with salt and pepper, then place on a large roasting tray over a medium–high heat and seal the beef on all sides. Remove from the roasting tray.

Place the carrots, celery and shallots with the thyme in the base of the roasting tray and sit the beef on top of the vegetables. Brush the beef with mustard all over and cook in the oven for 1 hour 45 minutes–2 hours.

Leave the beef to rest in a cool place for 30 minutes before carving and serving with the Yorkshire puddings, horseradish cream and some watercress.

CHOCOLATE

The general guideline for quality chocolate is the higher the percentage of cocoa solids the better. Cooking with chocolate can be a bit of an art form. In fact there are thousands of chocolatiers who work for big chocolate producers. The important thing is to be careful when you melt it as it can burn very easily. I find the easiest way is to first break it up into very small pieces or even grate it before placing it into a large bowl over some hot, but not boiling water. Using a spoon mix the chocolate constantly and allow it to melt slowly. The chocolate is now ready to use.

When choosing a chocolate try to buy an expensive one – you pretty much get what you pay for. Chocolate is an antioxidant. Dark chocolate, which has 70% or more cocoa solids, is the most nutritious form of chocolate. It is rich in potassium, magnesium and calcium.

● ○ ○

CHOCOLATE AND KAHLÚA FONDUE
WITH WINTER FRUITS

400 g/14 oz plain dark chocolate,
very finely chopped
500 ml/16 fl oz double cream
250 ml/8 fl oz Kahlúa
assorted fresh fruit and/or dessert
biscuits, such as biscotti,
to serve

serves 6–8 as a dessert

Talk about a blast from the past. I don't care what anyone says, this is still the perfect way not only to enjoy a delicious dessert but also to enjoy each others company. Sharing food is simply great with friends and family.

Place the chopped chocolate in a heatproof bowl. Heat the cream in a small saucepan until it is almost but not quite simmering. Once the cream is to near a simmer, very slowly pour it into the bowl of chocolate, stirring constantly.

Heat the Kahlúa in a separate saucepan to a near boil. Be careful as the liquid may ignite if it becomes too hot. Slowly add the Kahlúa to the chocolate and cream mixture and serve hot with fruit and biscuits for dipping.

FLOURLESS CHOCOLATE AND PECAN TORTE

This flourless chocolate torte is luscious and rich and works perfectly with the flavour of rum and pecan.

Preheat oven to 180ºC/350°F/Gas Mark 4. Grease and flour a 15 cm/6 inch cake tin. Cream the butter and sugar together in a large mixing bowl until light and fluffy. Add the egg yolks one at a time, then mix in the melted chocolate (see page 152), pecans and cinnamon.

Whisk the egg whites in a separate bowl until they form stiff peaks. Stir one-third of the egg whites into the chocolate mixture to loosen the texture, then, using a large metal spoon, fold in the remaining egg whites.

Transfer the mixture to the prepared cake tin.

Level the top with the back of a spoon and bake in the oven for 35–40 minutes. Leave to cool for at least 20 minutes, or until just slightly warm.

Meanwhile, warm the rum and sugar in a small saucepan and stir until dissolved. Remove from the heat and leave to cool before mixing in the crème fraîche. Semi-whip the double cream so it is still quite slack in a large bowl and fold through the crème fraîche mixture until fully blended.

Cut the torte into 8 equal-sized pieces and serve warm with the cream.

175 g/6 oz butter, softened, plus extra for greasing
plain flour, for dusting
175 g/6 oz caster sugar
6 eggs, separated
175 g/6 oz plain dark chocolate, melted
175 g/6 oz pecan nuts, finely chopped or coarsely processed
½ tsp ground cinnamon

For the cream
2 tbsp rum
2–3 tbsp muscovado (brown) sugar
100 ml/3½ fl oz crème fraiche
275 ml/9 fl oz double cream

serves 4–6

● ● ●   # CHOCOLATE AFTER-DINNER MINT

For the chocolate mousse

1 sheet gelatine

150 g/5 oz plain dark chocolate

2 small eggs

25 g/1 oz caster sugar

250 ml/8 fl oz double cream,
   semi-whipped

For the mint mousse

250 ml/8 fl oz full cream milk

80 g/3¼ oz caster sugar

1 bunch of fresh mint leaves

2 sheets gelatine

250 ml/8 fl oz whipping cream,
   semi-whipped

For the chocolate topping/ganache:

150 g/5 oz plain dark chocolate,
   grated

150 ml/5 fl oz double cream

fresh mint leaves, to decorate

serves 6–8, depending on
   size of serving glass

I must confess I have always been a sucker for the classic "After Dinner" mints. The combination of chocolate and mint is indulgent but still refreshing. While this dessert is a little time consuming none of the steps are very difficult and it's totally worth it!

To make the chocolate mousse:

Soften the gelatine in 250 ml/8 fl oz cold water. Melt the chocolate in a heatproof bowl set over a saucepan of hot water, stirring constantly.

Whisk the eggs and sugar in a mixing bowl with an electric whisk on medium–high speed until the eggs resemble medium peaks.

Place the softened gelatine in a small saucepan and melt over a low heat, then slowly add the gelatine to the eggs and sugar mixture, whisking constantly. Make sure that there are no lumps. Using a balloon whisk, slowly incorporate the melted chocolate (see page 152), then gently fold in the semi-whipped cream.

To make the mint mousse:

Bring the milk and sugar to the boil in a medium saucepan. Once boiling, add the mint leaves and whisk by hand for 20 seconds. Remove from the heat and cover with clingfilm. Set aside for 15 minutes.

Once the mint has infused with the milk and is still hot, add the softened gelatine and strain through a fine sieve into a bowl. Leave the milk to cool then add the semi-whipped cream (before the gelatine has set).

For the chocolate topping/ganache:

Place the grated chocolate in a heatproof bowl. Heat the double cream in a medium saucepan to a near simmer. Slowly pour the hot cream over the chocolate and stir. Once the chocolate has melted, leave to cool until it is slightly warmer than room temperature.

To assemble:

Place 2 tbsp of the chocolate mousse in the base of each serving glass and leave to set in the refrigerator for about 10–15 minutes.

Remove from the refrigerator and place 2 tbsp of the mint mousse on top of the chocolate mousse layer and return to the refrigerator to set for at least 30 minutes.

Pour a little chocolate ganache to cover the mint mousse layer, return to the refrigerator and leave to set for 10 minutes. Decorate the with mint leaves and serve after dinner.

INDEX

SUPPLIERS

*I get so inspired when
I come across ingredients
that have been produced
with a serious amount of
love, care and attention.
The people who have
supplied me in restaurants
for the past 7 years or so
have also supplied me with
the beautiful ingredients
you see in this book.
I admire and thank the
dedicated people who
care as much about food
as I do.*

Wild Harvest
Units B61-64
New Covent Garden Market
London SW8 5HH
Tel: 020 7498 5397
Fax: 020 7498 5419
www.wildharvestuk.com

Keltic Seafare (Scotland) Ltd
Unit 6
Strathpeffer Road Industrial
Estate
Dingwall
Rossshire IV15 9SP
Tel: 01349 864 087
Fax: 01349 866 394
www.kelticseafare.com

Nigel Fredericks
Nigel Fredericks House
Carlisle Road
Coindale
London NW9 0HD
Tel: 020 8905 9005
Fax: 020 8205 6151

Penbra Wyatts Fisheries Ltd
Salisbury Mews
Dawes Road
Fulham
London SW6 7DS
Tel: 020 7385 9693
Fax: 0207 381 8425

MG & Sons (Wholesale
Greengrocers) Ltd
D108-D111
Fruit & Vegetable Market
New Covent Garden Market
London SW8 5LL
Tel: 020 7720 8886
Fax: 020 7498 3041

Harrods
87-135 Brompton Road
Knightsbridge
London SW1 7XL
Tel: 020 7730 1234
Fax: 020 7581 0470
www.harrods.com

RD Baby Salad & Veg Ltd
23 Kendrick Close
Westbury
Wiltshire BA1 3QT
Tel: 0777 829 8121

La Credenza
Unit 16/59
Weir Road
London SW19 8UG
Tel: 020 7070 5070
Fax: 020 7070 5071

Blue Seafood Company
Unit 19-20
Torbay Business Park
Paignton
Devon TQ4 7HP
Tel: 01803 555 777

Live Langoustine Co. Ltd
Blackbrook Avenue
Paignton
Devon TQ4 7ND
Tel: 01803 843829

Top Catch
14, Cliff Rd
Paignton
Devon TQ4 6DG
Tel: 01803 520291

ACKNOWLEDGEMENTS

For my late granddad,
who was a market gardener and a bloody good cook.

I guess when it comes to my food, I'm a bit of a control freak about how it tastes and looks. The team that worked on this book not only gave me the freedom that I asked for, but also helped and inspired me every step of the way. So thanks and let's do it again some time … Kate Oldfield – Commissioning Editor, Emily Preece-Morrison – Editor and Jo Pratt – Home Economist.

A special thanks to the two women in my life: Martine Carter, my amazing agent and Katherine McIntosh, who at the last minute dropped everything to race over from Melbourne to London to help get everything out of my head and down on paper. Karzi, I'm eternally grateful and love ya loads.

Talking about bringing people from the other side of the world, it took some convincing, but photographer Craig Kinder and his partner Emma also came over from Australia and I'm sure you will agree have taken some of the most outstanding photography. Craig, thanks for your hard work mate – your shots speak for themselves.

Finally a chef is no-one without his or her loyal kitchen staff. I was lucky enough to have Pete Templeholf give me a hand testing recipes for a few days. Graham "Grumble" Towner who has been my sous chef and right hand man now for 4–5 years. Mate, you're a miserable bastard at times but in my mind you're a great chef and a dead set legend. I appreciate all your hard work.

First published in Great Britain in 2005 by
PAVILION BOOKS

An imprint of **Chrysalis** Books Group plc

The Chrysalis Building, Bramley Road, London W10 6SP
www.chrysalisbooks.co.uk

© Pavilion Books, 2005
Text © Curtis Stone, 2005
Photography © Craig Kinder, 2005,
except front cover image © Paul Dodds

The moral right of the author has been asserted.

COMMISSIONING EDITOR: Kate Oldfield
EDITOR: Emily Preece-Morrison
COPY EDITOR: Kathy Steer
DESIGNERS: Adelle Morris and Lotte Oldfield
PHOTOGRAPHER: Craig Kinder
PHOTOGRAPHER'S ASSISTANT: Emma Van Dordrecht
FOOD STYLING: Curtis Stone
HOME ECONOMIST: Jo Pratt
PROP STYLIST: Sara Emslie
INDEXER: Patricia Hymans

ISBN 1 86205 698 6

A CIP catalogue record for this book is available from the British Library.

10 9 8 7 6 5 4 3 2 1

Printer: Kyodo Printing Co Pte Ltd, Singapore
Reproduction: Anorax Imaging Ltd, England